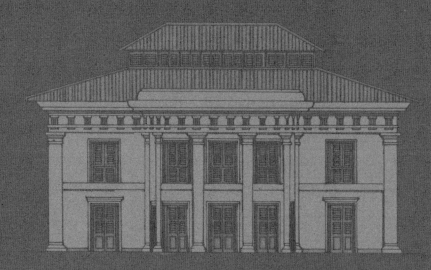

BLACK AND WHITE
THE SINGAPORE HOUSE 1898–1941

First Published in 2006
by Talisman Publishing Pte Ltd
52 Genting Lane #06-05 Ruby Land Complex 1
Singapore 349560

ISBN 981052739X

Publisher: Ian Pringle
Design & Layout: Chin Wei Woon, Talisman & Topographica
Copy Editor: Wu Xueyi

Typeset in VAG Rounded Thin, Helvetica
Printed and bound in Singapore by Saik Wah Press Pte Ltd

Captions for pp. i-xi:
Crest from Bididari Cemetery gates possibly designed by David McLeod Craik (p. i); House for R. Pears Esq., Chatsworth
Road, Swan & Maclaren (1913) (p. iii); Public Works Department bungalow, Malcolm Road (c.1925) (pp. iv-v); interior,
military black and white, Ridley Park (c.1920) (pp. vi-vii); Public Works Department bungalow, Goodwood Hill (C.1910)
(pp. viii-ix); Sub-Manager's house, Hongkong & Shanghai Banking Corporation, Mount Echo, Swan & Maclaren (1902)
(pp. x-xi)

BLACK AND WHITE
THE SINGAPORE HOUSE 1898–1941

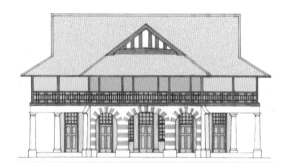

Julian Davison

PHOTOGRAPHY
Luca Invernizzi Tettoni

Talisman

HONGKONG & SHANGHAI BANKING CORPORATION.

SINGAPORE BRANCH.

PROPOSED NEW SUB-MANAGER'S HOUSE, MOUNT ECHO.

Jervois Rd.

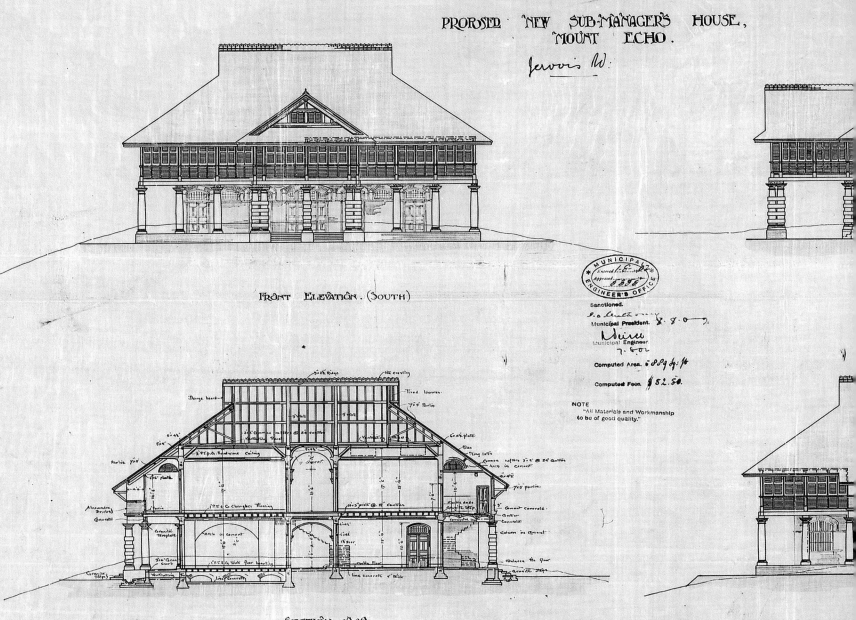

FRONT ELEVATION. (SOUTH)

SECTION. A.A.

SCALE, 8 FEET - 1 INCH.

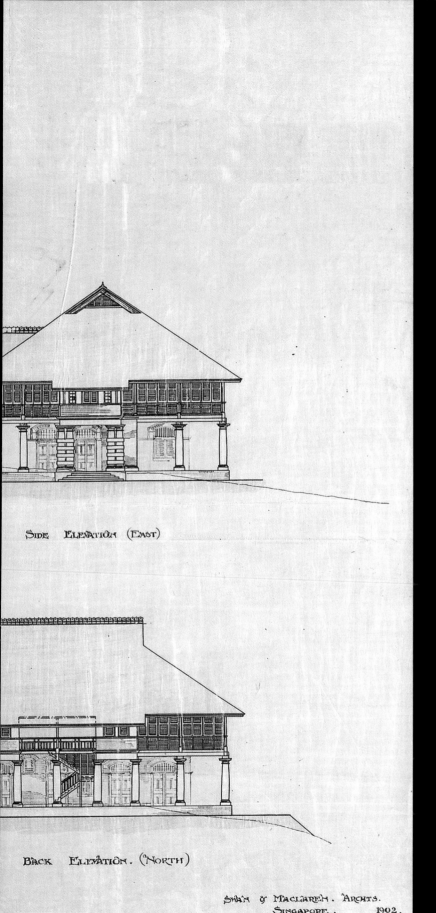

SIDE ELEVATION (EAST)

BACK ELEVATION. (NORTH)

SWAN & MACLAREN. ARCHTS.
SINGAPORE., 1902.

Contents

◆

INTRODUCTION

'Three conditions architecture must accomplish:
Utilitas (utility), Firmitas (permanence) and Venustas (beauty).'
— Marcus Vitruvius Pollio (fl. 46-30 BC), *De Architectura, Book 1* —

THE BLACK AND WHITE HOUSES OF SINGAPORE occupy a fascinating position in the architectural record of South East Asia. Not only do they represent a very singular architectural tradition, not found elsewhere in the region, but they also constitute an important legacy of the island's colonial past. With their stuccoed columns and half-timbered elevations, they encapsulate the quintessence of that bygone era, recalling charmed lives of ease and elegance. They are, however, much more than simply relics of Singapore's colonial period; these houses are also justly celebrated in purely architectural terms as representing a sensible and ecologically-sound response to the demands of designing for a tropical monsoon climate. Recent years have seen the emergence of a new kind of residential architecture in Asia, sometimes described as the tropical Asian house — an eclectic, post-Modernist mix of regional vernacular forms, which includes various borrowings from the domestic architecture of the colonial era. London educated Sri Lankan architect, the late Geoffrey Bawa, was the leading advocate of this new 'Asian vernacular' and his own residential work not only drew freely from his country's indigenous architecture, but also its colonial heritage — Portuguese, Dutch and British. The underlying idea here was that there were valuable design lessons to be learned from these existing architectures which had evolved, *in situ*, over centuries and which also were largely self-reliant on locally available materials and indigenous building technologies. The black and white Singapore house, which arose in precisely the same sort of

circumstances and similarly entails an amalgam of Western and local influences, is a part of this tradition, and in this respect their interest, architecturally speaking, reaches beyond the shores of Singapore island, and the historical moment in which they originated, to offer lessons in tropical design that continue to be relevant today.

❑

When it came to embarking upon the initial research for this book, I found to my surprise that there was not a great deal to be learned about black and white houses from the existing literature on the architecture of the colonial era. Lee Kip Lin, in his seminal study, *The Singapore House 1819–1942*, published in 1988, had curiously little to say on the subject other than to note that the "'Black-and-White' style was popular with government architects in the first four decades of the [last] century." Norman Edwards, in *The Singapore House and Residential Life 1819–1939*, which appeared a couple of years later, was hardly more forthcoming, though he did draw attention to the suitability of the black and white house "as a form of building appropriate to the Singaporean environment." Nor was there much information to be found in the academic literature, notably the late Professor E. J. Seow's doctoral dissertation, 'Architectural Development in Singapore', from the University of Melbourne (1973), and Jon Lim's block-buster PhD thesis 'Colonial Architecture and the Architects of Georgetown and Singapore between 1786 and 1942' — five volumes and more than 600 pages in length — submitted to the National

E. J. H. Corner House, Botanic Gardens.

Built in the 1920s, the house was once home to the Assistant Director of the Botanic Gardens, E. J. H. Corner, who worked at the gardens between 1929 and 1946. With its symmetrical plan, accented by a forward-projecting *porte cochère*, and brick-built ground floor, surmounted by a largely timber upper storey, the Corner House represents the quintessential elements of the black and white style.

University of Singapore in 1990. The general consensus of opinion of these authors was that the black and white house originated with the Public Works Department, or PWD as it was usually referred to, and was built to accommodate civil servants and other officers of the colonial administration on either side of the First World War, continuing through to the mid-thirties, by which time the style began to be superceded by more modern influences.

So far so good, but as I came to dig a little deeper into the origins and background of these houses, I found that there was a far richer and more interesting story to be told. This was mainly revealed by sifting through the huge number of housing plans submitted to the Municipality for planning permission during the half-century beginning around 1890 and continuing through to the advent of the war in the Pacific when the whole colonial enterprise came to a shuddering halt. These building plans are now lodged with the National Archives of Singapore in Coleman Street and after several months of winding through furlongs of microfilm, a whole new picture gradually began to emerge of which the PWD connection was just a part. What is more, it

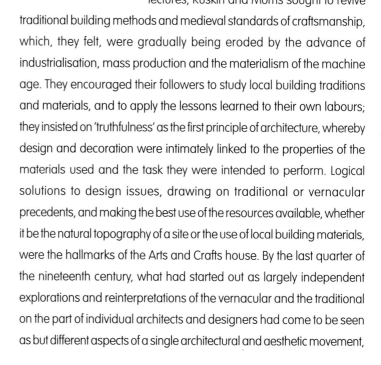
Tudor timber-frame house (late-fifteenth century).

also became apparent that in terms of their architectural import, the black and white houses of Singapore deserved far better recognition than they had hitherto received. The present study, which is nothing less than a celebration of the black and white era, aims to rectify this situation by explaining the origins of the style, its influences and antecedents, and the various transformations that it underwent with the passage of time. It is also an impassioned plea to preserve and conserve what remains of this remarkable legacy as an architectural treasure and historical icon that is unique to Singapore.

❑

The term 'black and white' derives from those houses built around the turn of the last century which incorporated elements of the so-called mock Tudor, or 'Tudorbethan' revival, style of architecture, which was at that time reaching the height of its popularity in England. The latter was characterised by half-timbered façades, sculpted bargeboards, 'Gothick'

finials and an assortment of other decorative embellishments loosely associated with traditional domestic architecture in England immediately prior to the English Renaissance and the introduction of Classical architecture from the Continent. This late-Victorian enthusiasm for fancy woodwork and 'magpie' façades — the timber elements were typically painted black and the rendered surfaces white — arose out of the same impulse that gave birth to the Gothic revival at the beginning of the nineteenth century, gathering impetus as the latter gradually extended its range of interests from the pointed arch and flying buttress of ecclesiastical architecture — there was a strong Christian imperative underlying the Gothic revival — to embrace vernacular forms and building methods. By the latter half of the Victorian era this passion for 'Old English' architecture as it was popularly known, disparate in its origins, had loosely come together as the Arts and Crafts movement, which coalesced around two leading protagonists, the art critic and Gothic proselytizer, John Ruskin, and his fellow medieval enthusiast, William Morris — craftsman, designer, poet, weaver, translator of Icelandic sagas, Utopian idealist and much else besides. Through their writings and lectures, Ruskin and Morris sought to revive traditional building methods and medieval standards of craftsmanship, which, they felt, were gradually being eroded by the advance of industrialisation, mass production and the materialism of the machine age. They encouraged their followers to study local building traditions and materials, and to apply the lessons learned to their own labours; they insisted on 'truthfulness' as the first principle of architecture, whereby design and decoration were intimately linked to the properties of the materials used and the task they were intended to perform. Logical solutions to design issues, drawing on traditional or vernacular precedents, and making the best use of the resources available, whether it be the natural topography of a site or the use of local building materials, were the hallmarks of the Arts and Crafts house. By the last quarter of the nineteenth century, what had started out as largely independent explorations and reinterpretations of the vernacular and the traditional on the part of individual architects and designers had come to be seen as but different aspects of a single architectural and aesthetic movement, which gradually extended its influence from buildings and furniture to embrace just about every aspect of creative design from bookbinding and typography to wallpaper and fabric — the term 'arts and crafts' was apparently coined by the bookbinder T. J. Cobden-Sanderson and acquired general currency after the newly-formed Arts and Crafts Exhibition Society held its inaugural show in the autumn of 1888.

❏

The earliest black and white houses were very much a product of the Arts and Crafts movement, manifest in the local context as a slightly surreal, hybrid style of architecture, perhaps best identified as tropical mock Tudor. In this last respect, the early black and white Singapore house, as a generic building type, was characterised by the extensive use of wood as a structural component. The ground floor was typically brick-built, while the upper storey comprised a load-bearing timber frame, which carried the roof, filled in with half-brick panels or nogging. Interestingly, in the original specifications, the timber frame was often left a natural wood

McAlister & Co. Mess, Cable Road, Swan & Maclaren (1920).

◆

colour, while other elements such as shutters and doors were typically painted a dark green — the ubiquitous black and white colour scheme was a later invention, it seems.

This type of construction technique had actually been around for a long time before the advent of the black and white house, having been employed in Singapore since at least the middle of the nineteenth century. And it is a very practical way to go about things — brick and plaster are much longer lasting than wooden boards, while timber framing is more economical than load-bearing masonry walls. Where the black and white house departed from its forbears was to turn this already existing construction technique into a stylistic feature which corresponded to the contemporary 'Tudorbethan' revivalist movement in England — the timber framework of the earliest black and white houses was quite consciously modelled on sixteenth-century references, though later there was less concern for historical fidelity. Stuccoed columns, broad verandahs and

widely-overhanging eaves completed the ensemble, which managed to combine the elegance of Classical architecture with a Jacobean rustic charm and at the same time was also very well suited to the local climate with its torrential rains alternating with harsh sunlight.

And this brings us to an important point. For all the apparent absurdity of trying to introduce a quasi-medieval style of architecture to the East Indies, the black and white house actually represents quite a sensible approach to the problem of designing for the tropics. The largely timber upper storey of the typical black and white house absorbs solar radiation less rapidly than a house built entirely of bricks and mortar, especially if the roof overhead was made of *atap* thatch as in the earliest examples. Conversely, the masonry ground floor with its tiled floors, protected from the direct heat of the sun by the wooden storey above, retains its nighttime coolness for much of the day. Verandahs and overhanging eaves also help to keep the heat of the sun from the core of the house and cut down glare. Rattan chicks and blinds let down in front of every verandah during the hottest hours of the day fulfill a similar function, but can be raised in the late afternoon or early evening to admit ambient breezes. Lastly, a high roof profile draws hot air from within the house into the roof cavity, to be dispersed by lateral vents — a kind of chimney-like system of natural ventilation. In each of these respects, the black and white house was well adapted to Singapore's equatorial monsoon climate, turning what might have been simply a stylistic exercise — a local parody of the Tudorbethan revival back in England — into a domestic architecture that was at once charming and also well suited to the environment.

Some of these elements had been introduced to Singapore from British India; others had evolved *in situ*. In the two hundred years or so since the Honourable East India Company (EIC) had first obtained permission from the Moghul court to establish a factory at Hugli, the English had learnt a thing or two from the indigenous people of Bengal, and one of them was the bungalow style of architecture. The term bungalow derives from the Hindustani *bangala*, meaning 'of, or belonging to, Bengal' and actually describes a fairly rudimentary kind of indigenous dwelling in those parts. Once, however, the basic model had been suitably modified to reflect the dignity of an official in the service of the Honourable Company, the Anglo-Indian bungalow, with its characteristic verandahs and broad, shady eaves, was universally adopted as the standard type of dwelling for an Englishman abroad in hot and sticky climes, which naturally included Singapore in the very earliest days of the Settlement.

Later, as the British established themselves more securely on the island, we see a second import from India, a gracious, neo-Classical style of architecture, sometimes described as Anglo-Indian Regency. Irishman, George Drumgoolde Coleman (1795-1846), the first, and for a long time the only, professionally-trained architect to have practiced in Singapore, was the man responsible for the latter introduction. Coleman, who had previously practiced in Dublin and Calcutta, was a man of many parts. He worked with Singapore's founder, Sir Stamford Raffles on the first Town Planning Ordinances of 1822-23; he surveyed and laid out many of the early streets and thoroughfares; and he also designed some very fine

Caldwell House, Victoria Street, George Coleman (1840/41)

buildings in the neo-Classical manner, a few of which have survived to this day. They include the Armenian Church in Hill Street and Caldwell House in the Convent of the Holy Infant Jesus complex (today's Chijmes), as well as the core portion of Old Parliament House which started life as a private residence. Of all his many exertions, it was undoubtedly Coleman's Regency-style houses for well-to-do merchants which proved to be the most significant of his labours in Singapore in that they established architectural precedents that were to influence the domestic architecture of the island's wealthy elite until well into the next century.

The typical Coleman house was a two-storey affair, symmetrical in plan, in the Palladian manner, with a forward-projecting portico, or *porte cochère*, augmented by a Classical pediment and frieze. The principal living rooms were on the first floor, or *piano nobile* (the term comes from Palladio), while the ground floor was reserved for offices and storage. His early houses had a flat roof in the Anglo-Indian Regency style — the so-called Madras flat-top — but in his later work he opted for a pitched roof with extended eaves. A sloping roof was clearly much better adapted to Singapore's torrential rains than the ill-suited Madras flat-top, while the overhanging eaves served to shade the external walls from the full heat of the sun, reducing the solar radiation that they absorbed and keeping the interior of the house cool. Together, they represented a first step forward towards a more tropical kind of architecture for Singapore.

Coleman's influence on the development of the colonial house in Singapore cannot be over-emphasised and for fifty years after his death in 1846 the generously-proportioned, Palladian-style villa represented the *beau-ideal* of a gentleman's domicile in Singapore, synonymous with a lifestyle that was at once "ineffably and exclusively British, but one modified by the Anglo-Indian experience." But there were other influences at work too, not least that of the local vernacular in the form of the Malay house — a roof of *atap* thatch was a cheap but serviceable alternative to tiles, while a living floor raised on stilts made good sense in a damp and humid climate where sudden inundations were a daily part of life.

Coleman was a professionally-trained architect who had served his apprenticeship in the elegant Georgian city of Dublin, but those who followed him were not always of the same calibre and from the 1840s onwards, the Singapore house was very much left in the hands of amateurs. Major public buildings were the responsibility of the Government Engineer, who was usually a military man with a formal training in mechanics and at least a basic understanding of the rudiments of neo-Classical architecture, which was very much the imperial style. Private houses, on the other hand, were thrown up by just about anyone who had a mind to, chiefly building contractors and the odd dilettante or architect manqué. They drew their inspiration, not from the fount of architectural knowledge, acquired through years of pupillage and laborious study of the ancients, but rather from pattern books — nineteenth-century design manuals — which provided them with templates for just about any kind of built structure from a privy to a triumphal arch. The pattern book may have been a God-send for the beleaguered military engineer, working with coolie or convict labour under a blazing tropic sun, somewhere east of Suez, but in other hands the results, it must be said, were often a less than qualified success.

By the end of the nineteenth century, the Singapore house had departed quite some way from the elegant tropical Palladianism of Coleman — it was comfortable and commodious, and not altogether displeasing to the eye, but it lacked the rigour of a building designed by someone with a formal architectural training. The basic plan had remained the same for more than half a century — symmetrical, in the Classical manner, with a forward-projecting *porte cochère*, the legacy of Coleman's original prototype — but any notion of Classical orders or Palladian proportion had died with Coleman. And where the modest suburban villa made do with fluted Corinthian columns and perhaps a row of green-glazed Venetian balusters, the more extravagant erections of the rich literally erupted in a frenzy of surface decoration — a riotous assembly of swags and festoons, garlands and escutcheons, which Northcote Parkinson — he of Parkinson's Law fame — once described as "Chinese Baroque Mannerism".

It is at this point that the black and white house suddenly emerges upon the scene and for the first time since the august days of Coleman half a century earlier, we see at work the hand of a professionally-qualified architect — a man who knew his Vetruvius from his Palladio, his Wren from his Hawksmoor, a man who no doubt had read his Ruskin and William Morris and more importantly knew all about the latest architectural trends in England. That man was one Regent Alfred John Bidwell (1869–1918).

House for Tan Kee Pek, Killiney Road (c.1880s).

Bidwell embarked upon an architectural career early in life — at seventeen he was already enrolled at the prestigious Architectural Association in Bedford Square, London, where he won an award for design. He studied for his articles with a London firm and after qualifying worked for a number of other practices in the city, eventually winding up Assistant to the Superintending Architect of the London County Council. During this early part of his career he taught at the Architectural Association and was also its joint secretary for a while. Then, some time in the early 1890s, Bidwell left London and headed East to join the Public Works Department in Kuala Lumpur, in the Malayan state of Selangor, which was then being developed by the British as their administrative capital for the Malay Peninsula. The big project that he worked on there was the Government Secretariat, today's Sultan Abdul Samad Building, which was completed 1896. The original plans for the building were drawn up by Bidwell, under the supervision of State Architect, A. C. Norman, and were Classical in manner, which was generally accepted as the style best suited to representing British imperial governance. State Engineer and PWD Director, C. E. Spooner, approved of the layout, but felt that something a little more 'Oriental' would befit the building's situation and purpose and asked Norman to reconsider his original design. Although, the Government Secretariat is officially attributed to Norman, the general consensus of opinion is that it was Bidwell who actually came up with the remarkable Victorian 'Moorish' or Indo-Saracenic-Gothic elevations that we see today.

In 1895, Bidwell quit the PWD in Malaya and moved to Singapore to join the architectural practice of Swan & Maclaren, which had then been in existence some ten years. At Swan & Maclaren, he quickly established himself as the firm's leading player, becoming a partner in 1899. Bidwell was the Coleman of his day and by the time he left the Swan & Maclaren in 1911 to practice on his own, he had designed some of Singapore's best known landmarks including Raffles Hotel

(1899 and 1904), the Teutonia Club (today's Goodwood Park Hotel) (1900), the Chased-el Synagogue (1905), the Victoria Memorial Hall (1906) and the Singapore Cricket Club (1907). He was also responsible for a string of prestigious houses for the good and the great of Singapore, and among them we find the very earliest tropical mock Tudor mansions to be built in the colony. The first of these, Atbara, for barrister John Burkinshaw at Gallop Road (see pp. 24-29), dates from 1898, and is a fairly tentative stab at the mock Tudor idiom. It is not until some five or six years later that Bidwell achieves his fully mature black and white style with his magisterial Tudorbethan mansion for W. Patchitt in 1903 (p.37), or his more modest, almost cottage-like, black and white for Captain G. Kinghorn the following year. Up until that time, Bidwell was without imitators and so one can say, with a fair degree of certainty, that he was the originator of the black and white style.

The important thing about Bidwell, aside from his undeniable talent, was that he was up to date with the latest architectural trends in England. As a former secretary of the Architectural Association, he would have been familiar with the work of the most prominent architects of his day — at least until the 1890s when he left for the East — and he would definitely have been well acquainted with the

House for Captain G. Kinghorn, R. A. J. Bidwell (1904).

◆

architecture of Richard Norman Shaw (1831–1913) who was perhaps the leading British architect in the last three decades of the nineteenth century, certainly when it came to residential work.

Shaw, like several other prominent architects of his generation, started out as a draftsman in the offices of Victorian Gothicist George Edmund Street, from whom he acquired a deep-felt respect for traditional craftsmanship, materials and building techniques. This early enthusiasm led him to make a study of the English vernacular, based on field trips to Yorkshire, Kent and Sussex, and the material that he collected during the course of these expeditions stood him in good stead when he came to going it alone. After leaving Street in 1862, Shaw set himself up in partnership with William Eden Nesfield. Nesfield had accompanied Shaw on some of his field trips, and together they set out to create a modern vernacular, which in time came to be identified as 'Old English'. The term had of course already been used at a slightly earlier period in time to describe traditional English domestic architecture prior to the advent of Classicism, but where Shaw and Nesfield departed from the work of their predecessors was in their daring combination of traditional elements to create a new and slightly fantastic architecture of their own.

An eclectic mix of Gothic arches, half-timbered façades, mullioned windows, soaring brick chimneystacks, panelled interiors and cosy inglenooks gives a fairly good idea of the extravagance of Shaw's imagination in this respect, scorning stylistic correctness as he blazed his way to a new vernacular — a vernacular that was built on traditional elements to be sure, but which combined them in novel and original ways. In doing so, Shaw demonstrated that the vernacular had a place in modern architecture and that the past could be reinterpreted, reinvented even, in terms of the new.

Old English was hugely popular, especially with the newly rich looking to build themselves a house in the country that was at once modern yet at the same time positively bristled with traditional features, and from the late 1860s onwards Shaw was greatly in demand. Perspectives of his latest work were regularly published in the architectural press and his drawings were exhibited each year at the Royal Academy. The invention of photolithography around this time meant that Shaw's own pen-and-ink perspectives could be easily reproduced, which only added to his fame both at home and abroad — a few years earlier and it would have been necessary to laboriously turn these images into engravings, which would almost certainly have meant that far fewer of them would have been reproduced for publication. These improved reproduction techniques helped to spread Shaw's 'new vernacular' across North America and no doubt also brought him to the notice of architects and other interested parties elsewhere in the world. Certainly in Singapore, one can definitely detect the influence of Shaw on local architects towards the end of the nineteenth century, not least in the work of R. A. J. Bidwell.

This is perhaps best seen in two early houses by Bidwell, from 1897, on the White House Park estate between Stevens Road and Whitley Road. Named Glencaird and Glen Cree respectively, they were commissioned by John Fraser, one of the founders of the aerated drinks company Fraser & Neave, and they were both considerable late-Victorian piles. More to the point, they both departed radically from the typical late-nineteenth-century house in Singapore in their rejection of classical symmetry in favour of an asymmetrical plan, accentuated by a dramatic, turret-like, three-storey stair hall to one side. Glencaird and Glen Cree were also unusual for Singapore at that time in their eclectic use of materials and architectural elements which included expanses of unrendered brickwork, quoins, and rusticated archways with huge, white-stuccoed voussoirs. These were favourite devices of Bidwell, used to good effect in several other buildings designed by him, most notably the Teutonia Club of 1900 and his Singapore Cricket Club extension of 1907, but they also call to mind Shaw's 'streaky bacon' style of the 1880s, which similarly alternated sections of exposed brickwork with bands

Glen Cree, White House Park, R. A. J. Bidwell (1897).

of white stucco. (Throughout his career, Shaw periodically reinvented himself: he started out as a Gothicist, then came Old English, followed by Queen Anne — a loose neo-Classical style that combined Dutch gables, Tuscan columns and Georgian, segmentally-headed sash windows — after which there was streaky bacon, and lastly a kind of Edwardian Baroque in the early years of the new century.) More significant, as far as our present interests are concerned, is the revelation from the working drawings that the rear elevation of Glen Cree also included a half-timbered gable. At the time, the latter, so casually deployed, was probably seen as no more than an amusing gesture in the manner of Shaw, but viewed in retrospect it acquires a special import as a sign of what was to come. Indeed, one could argue that the archetypal black and white house, with its neo-Classical ground floor and half-timbered upper storey — a combination of

Queen Anne and Old English — was exactly what Shaw himself might have proposed had he been asked to design a suburban villa for the tropics. Shaw, without doubt, was a major influence on the genesis of the black and white house.

Bidwell was one of the first professionally-trained architects to practice in Singapore, but from 1902, the Municipality and Public Works Department insisted on the presentation of professional qualifications when recruiting in order to help raise the standard of architecture in the colony. This brought the likes of Scotsman David McLeod Craik, Charles Williams, William Draper and Vincent Steadman to Singapore, all of whom were members of the Royal Institute of British Architects and all of whom started out by working either for the Municipality or PWD. Subsequently, they left the government to go into private practice, either on their own or in partnership, and together they played a major role in the development of the black and white style in the years leading up to the First World War. The point to note here is that like Bidwell, this new breed of

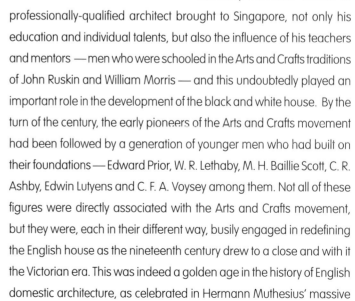

professionally-qualified architect brought to Singapore, not only his education and individual talents, but also the influence of his teachers and mentors — men who were schooled in the Arts and Crafts traditions of John Ruskin and William Morris — and this undoubtedly played an important role in the development of the black and white house. By the turn of the century, the early pioneers of the Arts and Crafts movement had been followed by a generation of younger men who had built on their foundations — Edward Prior, W. R. Lethaby, M. H. Baillie Scott, C. R. Ashby, Edwin Lutyens and C. F. A. Voysey among them. Not all of these figures were directly associated with the Arts and Crafts movement, but they were, each in their different way, busily engaged in redefining the English house as the nineteenth century drew to a close and with it the Victorian era. This was indeed a golden age in the history of English domestic architecture, as celebrated in Hermann Muthesius' massive three-volume tome, *Das Englische Haus* (1904-1905). It was a moment when British design led the world — the Arts and Crafts movement was the first 'International Style' — and the architects who came out East at the turn of the century simply brought it with them. And without doubt it was the advent of the professionally-qualified architect in Singapore — Bidwell and those who came after him — which, more than anything else, was the impetus that gave rise to the birth and subsequent development of the black and white house.

❏

Ultimately, the era of the black and white house was relatively short-lived — no more than twenty-five years in all. The first appeared on the cusp of the nineteenth century and by the mid-twenties the original inspiration for the black and white house had more or less exhausted itself. The Golden Era of the black and white house, though, came shortly before the end, just after the First World War when the rapid revival of Singapore's economy led to a property boom in 1919/1920. By this time, Bidwell had disappeared from the scene, dead at the early age of forty-eight. Possibly he suffered from some protracted illness, because in 1909 he had stepped down as partner with Swan & Maclaren, though somewhat mysteriously he remained with the firm as a staff architect until 1912, before going out on his own. By then there were only half-a-dozen commissions to come, Bidwell's last major work being a house for Dr. D. J. Galloway at Cairnhill in 1913.

In 1919, a huge number of new houses were commissioned, not only by wealthy individuals who were doing well out of the resumption of normal trading relations in the immediate postwar period, but also by the corporate sector. Singapore businesses were doing well in an increasingly globalised economy and long-established British firms, as well as a new breed of multi-nationals such as the Firestone Tire Company and British American Tobacco, were looking to provide accommodation for their expanding European staff and a clutch of black

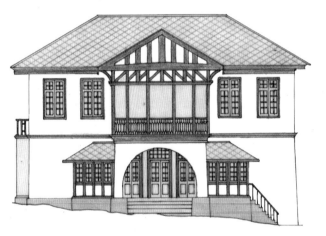

British American Tobacco Co., Nassim Road, Swan & Maclaren (1920).

◆

and white houses set down in a leafy enclave somewhere in the Tanglin area was ideally suited to their needs. New residential estates for civil servants were also being built by the government around this time as Singapore's colonial administration similarly grew in size in the immediate postwar era. The houses for the latter were designed by the Public Works Department and 'black and white' continued to be the department's 'house style', in every sense, right up until the Pacific war.

In the private sector, though, it was a different story and by the mid-twenties the black and white house had more or less had its day — tastes were changing and a new generation of postwar architects was taking the Singapore house in other directions. The houses of Frank Brewer and a few like-minded contemporaries, most notably the former Municipal Engineer, John MacBride Jackson, are an exception, and kept alive the flame of the Arts and Crafts movement in Singapore until the Japanese Occupation. The influences, however, were rather different from those that had launched the prewar black and white house, the principal source of inspiration this time around being the architecture of C. F. A. Voysey, particularly his later houses from around the turn of the century. Voysey was as fashionable in his day as Shaw had been a quarter of a century before, but he was a very different sort of fellow. While remaining true to his Arts and Crafts origins in terms of architectural integrity and the honest use of materials, Voysey favoured a relatively straightforward, no-nonsense approach to design. There was none of Shaw's faux-medievalism; rather Voysey's houses were characterised by relatively plain and unornamented façades, with buttressed walls and small windows tucked up under the eaves, surmounted by a dramatic expanse of roof which flared out slightly at the base. Some architectural historians have seen in this simpler, less fussy, stripped-down vernacular style, the forerunner of Modernism and there may be some truth in this because Brewer, in his non-residential work, was an out-and-out Modernist, being responsible for the late, lamented Cathay Building (1939), Singapore's first 'skyscraper' (demolished 2004).

Although the era of the classic black and white house had run its course by the late twenties, there was a last recrudescence of the basic formula in the years immediately before the Second World War, when the British Government embarked upon long-delayed plans to turn Singapore into their principal naval base east of Suez and there was a flurry of house building to provide accommodation for the influx of naval and military personnel. Some might argue that these later military 'black and whites' are not black and white houses in the strictest sense of the term, but they clearly owe an allegiance to the classic black and white bungalows designed by the Public Works Department in the early twenties, and in this respect they can be seen as a late flowering of the black and white tradition. Moreover, they constitute a sizeable portion of those black and white houses that survive to this day, for the sad fact is that by far the great majority of black and white houses that were built in the first three decades of the last century are no longer in existence. They were privately owned and long ago made way for the redevelopment of the sites on which they once stood. The military black and whites, on the other hand, together with those built by the Public Works Department for the colonial administration, managed to escape destruction because they formerly belonged to British government and when Singapore gained her independence in 1963 they were handed over, lock, stock and barrel, to the in-coming administration, which has retained them as a kind of upmarket government housing pool.

House for Mohamed Hussain, Haig Road, J. M. Jackson (1925).

Generally speaking, these government-owned houses have been well-maintained, though unfortunately many of their original features have been lost or else considerably altered over the years through unsympathetic 'restorations' and refurbishments. This can always be rectified. More worryingly, the few private black and white houses that remain — and this includes Atbara — are in very poor condition and in need of urgent attention. It is hoped that this book will go some way to alerting their present owners to the architectural treasures that they have in their possession.

Today, the black and white house is synonymous with the idea of an Englishman's home in Singapore during the colonial era. Their importance, however, extends beyond the merely historical — they are actually damn good houses to live in. Ultimately, though, they were very much a product of their time and in this respect they are both singular and precious. On the one hand, they reflected contemporary architectural fashions and enthusiasms imported from Europe at the tail end of the nineteenth century and in this context they were regarded as innovative, revolutionary even, in relation to the existing residential architecture of colonial Singapore. But at the same time, they were also very much a homegrown creation — the architects who designed these houses were more than willing to incorporate lessons learned from India as well as local architectural traditions in their response to the demands of designing sensible houses for a tropical climate. In doing so, they managed to create a singular style of tropical architecture that was at once quintessentially English, yet at the same time unmistakably Eastern. And it is this combination of the familiar and the exotic which, perhaps more than anything else, is what really bestows upon the black and white house its unusual charm, rather like finding an English rose growing in a bed of Heliconias.

OUT OF INDIA
ANGLO-INDIAN INFLUENCES

THE BLACK AND WHITE HOUSE did not suddenly appear on the scene, fully-formed and without antecedents, but rather was built upon an existing architectural tradition that was already well established in Singapore by the end of the nineteenth century. Many characteristic features of the black and white house such as broad verandahs, high ceilings, tall jalousie windows and widely overhanging eaves, were all part of the local architectural lexicon long before the first black and white houses came to be built. They came from India, where the British had been established since the early part of the seventeenth century and had evolved their own unique style of domestic architecture — the Anglo-Indian bungalow. Subsequently exported to every corner of the globe courtesy of the British Empire, the bungalow was introduced to Singapore with the founding of the East India Company's new trading post on the island by Sir Stamford Raffles in 1819.

◀ Dr. McKinnon's residence, Prince of Wales Island (c.1812); chromolithograph, taken from an original sketch by James Wathen.

Dr. McKinnon's Penang residence, foursquare in plan, with a pyramidal roof of local thatch and verandahs on all sides, reveals a close affinity with contemporary Anglo-Indian bungalows in British India, save for the fact that the latter were more likely to have been single-storey structures. This is pretty much as one might expect, given that most of the early British merchants and pioneers who settled Penang and Singapore had previously served with the East India Company in Bengal and other parts of India.

The Colonial Bungalow

The colonial house, in Singapore as well as in every other far-flung corner of the British Empire, begins and ends with the bungalow. Strictly speaking, a bungalow is a single-storey dwelling, but as one-time editor of *The Straits Times*, John Cameron, observes in *Our Tropical Possessions in Malayan India* (1865), the term is "... often applied to any style of dwelling-house in the East." I suspect that the reason for this lies partly in what might properly be described as *the* defining feature of bungalow architecture, namely the verandah; if every bungalow has a verandah, then equally every house with a verandah shares some of the qualities of a bungalow.

The verandah was the main living area in the colonial home, an intermediate space between the outside world and the inner sanctum of the house, a place for entertaining guests, writing letters home, or simply relaxing with a cup of tea. In the popular imagination it has acquired an iconic status, inseparable from the image of the stoic Englishman, dressed for dinner, with a smouldering cheroot in one hand and a glass of whiskey in the other, watching the sun go down on another day of tireless empire-building in a hot and heathen land. As Jan Morris observes, in her *Stones of Empire: the Buildings of British India*, "As long as the British in India are remembered at all, they will be remembered against the background of the bungalow, taking sundowners on its vevandah [and] playing badminton on its lawns."

▲ No. 1 Winchester Road, Alexandra Park (mid-1930s).

Built for the army in the buildup to the war in the Pacific, this black and white bungalow on the former military estate of Alexandra Park, exemplifies the evolved bungalow form in Singapore and the Straits Settlements, a century and more after its introduction from British India.

▼ Verandah living in British India, from *Curry and Rice (on Forty Plates), or the Ingredients of Social Life at "Our" Station in India,* by Captain George Francklin Atkinson (1859).

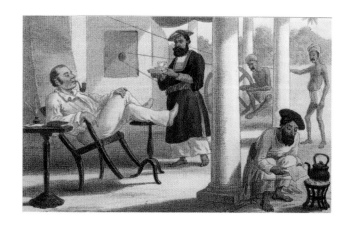

A Bungalow for an Electrician

Junior Electrician's bungalow, Morse Road (c.1915).

The original, locally-manufactured Chinese roof tiles have since been replaced by corrugated zinc sheets; the use of zinc sheeting as a roofing material dates back to the end of the nineteenth century and was regularly used as such for contemporary bungalows in Australia and Africa.

Built for the Eastern Extension Australasia & China Telegraph Co. (forerunner of today's Cable & Wireless), the bungalow shown here is typical of the more modest Anglo-Malay style of bungalow that was once such a characteristic feature of the Singapore and the Malayan landscape. Erected around the time of the First World War, it was designed by the firm of Swan & Maclaren, at that time the premier architectural practice in Singapore. The plan is symmetrical, with two bedrooms placed on either side of a central dining room and a forward projecting 'lounge verandah'. The bathrooms are at the rear and the kitchen and servants' quarters are detached from the main body of the house, to which they are connected by a covered walkway. All these elements can ultimately be traced back to the Anglo-Indian bungalow of British India. Where these houses depart from the Anglo-Indian prototype is the elevated floor which is raised off the ground on masonry piers — evidence of the influence of traditional Malay architecture.

The Earliest Houses

An early sketch of Singapore town from the sea by Lieutenant Philip Jackson, dated 5 June 1823, shows the very first houses built by Europeans soon after the Settlement was founded. They are all single-storey, timber buildings, fronted by long verandahs, with high thatched roofs, some of them pyramidal, others hipped. In some instances, there is a projecting porch at the front, with additional verandahs running down the sides. They resemble the earliest European houses in Penang, or Prince of Wales Island as it was known then, which had been established as an East India Company trading post some thirty-five years earlier, in 1786. Sketches made by the artist James Wathen, who visited Penang in 1811–12, show two houses built around the turn of the century. Dr. McKinnon's residence (see pp. 10-11), with its pyramidal roof and surrounding verandah, is clearly modelled on the contemporary Anglo-Indian bungalow of British India, which is much as one might expect, given that many of the Englishmen who settled Penang and later Singapore had previously served with the East India Company in Bengal; they simply brought the idea with them, making do with whatever local building materials were available. Mr. Amee's house, on the other hand, shows the influence of local Malay architecture, being raised on stilts with an enclosed verandah. Both the Anglo-Indian bungalow and the Malay house were to have a formative influence on the evolution of the Singapore house during the early-to-mid- nineteenth century and ultimately inform the black and white house as well.

▲ Singapore Town; original pencil sketch by Lt. Philip Jackson (1823) (detail).

This early sketch of Singapore in its infancy shows how the European town had developed along the shoreline to the north of the river mouth in the first five years of settlement. Most of the houses can be seen to be Anglo-Indian style bungalows, built of wood with pyramidal or hipped roofs thatched with *atap*.

▼ The house of Mr. Amee, Prince of Wales Island; original pencil sketch by James Wathen (c.1812).

Here we see the early genesis of two characteristic features of the Anglo-Malay bungalow, namely the main living floor being raised up off the ground on stilts and the addition of a centrally-placed entrance porch projecting forward from the main body of the house.

Malay Influences

▲ Traditional Malay house, Singapore (c.1900).

▼ A house for S. Reid Esq., at Syed Alley Road (1897).
Although contemporary with the first black and white houses, which began to appear around the end of the nineteenth century, Mr. Reid's Malay-style bungalow on Syed Alley Road (today's Newton Road), with its *atap* roof and mainly timber construction, looks back to the earliest days of the Settlement.

The first British settlers in Singapore started out by building houses for themselves in the style that they were already familiar with in India, but in time they began to include one or two local features which are not found on the subcontinent. One important difference between the Singapore bungalow and its Anglo-Indian forebears is that while the latter were built, in the Indian manner, on a raised plinth of hardcore rubble or compressed earth, their Singapore derivatives were elevated a few feet off the ground on brick piers. This allowed the through circulation of air underneath the house, ventilating the wooden floors and generally alleviating the humidity within the house. It also safeguarded against attacks from termites on an otherwise largely timber structure and could be useful in times of inundation, which, given Singapore's damp and rainy monsoon climate, were not uncommon. This innovation was almost certainly borrowed from traditional Malay architecture, where houses are raised on wooden posts, or stilts, for much the same reasons — the earliest houses erected by the British in Penang and later Singapore were no doubt built by Malay craftsmen, and perhaps it was they who first suggested the idea to the strange new arrivals from overseas.

The Anglo-Malay Bungalow

The first houses erected by the British in Singapore were very like those they were accustomed to building back in India; that is to say, single-storey bungalows with high pyramidal or hipped roofs, constructed from local building materials. These were quick and easy to put up and were well suited to the vicissitudes of the tropical climate. However, after a second treaty with the Sultan of Johor, in 1824, ceded the island of Singapore in its entirety to the East India Company *in perpetua*, those with money were encouraged to build more substantial homes for themselves, with brick foundations and tiled roofs. Classical columns lent a quiet dignity to these later bungalows, while simultaneously endorsing the Englishman's sense of himself at the top of the social hierarchy.

John Cameron, one-time editor of *The Straits Times*, has left us with this description of the typical Anglo-Malay bungalow in Singapore in the mid-1860s: "Bungalows … are properly speaking, only of one storey, elevated some five or six feet from the ground upon arched masonry. A moderate-sized building of this description might be 90 feet long, 60 or 70 deep, usually a parallelogram [i.e. rectangular] in form, but sometimes varied in shape to suit the arrangement of rooms inside. The walls from the floor to the ceiling are seldom less than fifteen feet high, which gives a lofty ceiling to the apartments, and the roof is covered with tiles."

"The most striking feature of these buildings," adds Cameron , "is the broad verandah which runs right round the house about eight or ten feet in width, resting on the plinths of the pillars that, extending upwards in round columns with neatly moulded capitals, support the continuation of the roof which projects some four feet beyond the pillars, forming deep overhanging eaves."

▼ Bungalow for the Peninsular & Oriental Steam Navigation Company (P&O), at Keppel Harbour (1900).

Although the P&O bungalow dates from 1900, the layout and elevation exemplify the typical Anglo-Malay bungalow of the 1860s as described by John Cameron. Note in particular the colonnaded verandah extending round all four sides of the central core of the building, providing protection from the monsoon rains and the heat and glare of the harsh tropical sunshine in equal measures.

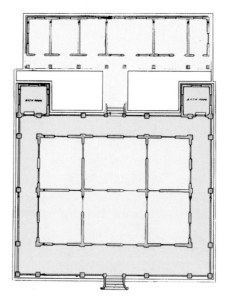

An East Coast Vernacular

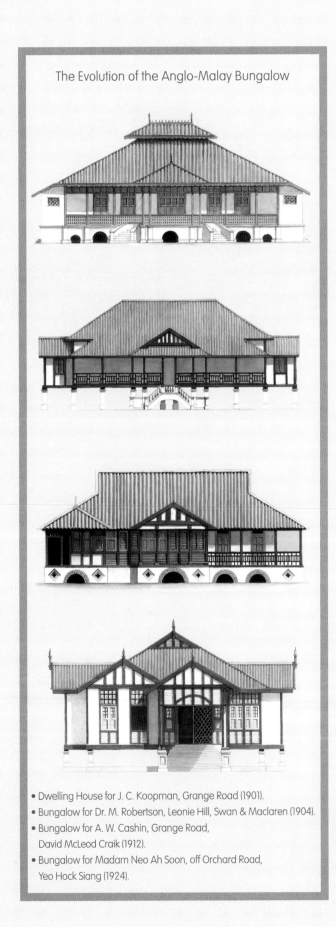

The Evolution of the Anglo-Malay Bungalow

- Dwelling House for J. C. Koopman, Grange Road (1901).
- Bungalow for Dr. M. Robertson, Leonie Hill, Swan & Maclaren (1904).
- Bungalow for A. W. Cashin, Grange Road, David McLeod Craik (1912).
- Bungalow for Madam Neo Ah Soon, off Orchard Road, Yeo Hock Siang (1924).

▼ Typical East Coast bungalow from around 1930 — a timber-frame structure built over a masonry base, with an asymmetrical plan and picturesque turret to one side.

The single-storey Anglo-Malay bungalow, raised a little off the ground on masonry piers, remained a popular house form well into the twentieth century. A Major Low, recording his impressions of Singapore in 1840, noted that although there were plenty of "handsome" two-storey houses, "old Indians [i.e. Company men who had previously served in India] are apt to prefer the bungalow style on the score of their superior coolness."

Later versions eschewed the classical symmetry of the Anglo-Indian prototype in favour of more whimsical or picturesque layouts, reflecting the influence of the Arts and Crafts movement, but the basic elements — a raised floor, broad verandahs, extended eaves and plenty of double-leafed doors for good through ventilation — remained in place until the advent of the war in the Pacific.

Large numbers of half-timbered, Anglo-Malay-style bungalows were built in the East Coast suburbs of Geylang, Tanjong Katong and Telok Kurau in the years before the Second World War. The latter were mostly designed by Asian architects for Asian or Eurasian clients. No doubt the fact that it was relatively economical to build in this way added to the longevity of the style, but it should not be thought that just because these homes were cheap to construct, they were necessarily nasty. On the contrary, though modest in extent, these East Coast houses are often extremely charming, with all sorts of quirky embellishments, including a fondness for chateau-style turrets, that put one in mind of the much-celebrated Californian bungalow style that grew up in the San Francisco Bay area more or less around the same period in time.

Suburban Villas

The group of four surviving bungalows on Scotts Road was built as part of a single development in the late 1920s. This was a period which saw a rapid growth of Singapore's suburbs, reflecting the prosperity of the immediate postwar years. As land prices near the centre of town began to increase dramatically, the large gardens and grounds of earlier houses were subdivided into smaller plots and sold off either individually or in batches to property developers, much as one sees happening in the outer suburbs today. These more modest homes for Singapore's burgeoning Asian and Eurasian middle classes, reflected the ambitions and aspirations of their upwardly mobile occupants and there was a tendency to rather over egg the cake. The four bungalows on Scotts Road are a case in point, the hugely inappropriate Corinthian columns of the two left-hand properties being completely out of scale with the rest of the house and more than a little vulgar in their pretension. However, the two bungalows on the right, with their more modest detailing and delicate use of the Doric order, get it just about right and in a curious way bring to mind Thomas Jefferson's miniaturised Classicism at Monticello.

◀▼ The Anglo-Malay bungalow reinvented; Scotts Road development (late 1920s). Singapore's strong postwar economy in the 1920s led to an influx of European expatriates and at the same time encouraged the growth of a local Asian and Eurasian middle class. It also saw the advent of the property speculator-cum-developer. Then as now, the architectural sensibilities of the latter were contentious, the principal interest here being the pursuit of profit rather than the aesthetically sublime. In the case of the Scotts Road bungalows, where the left-hand pair (left) try too hard to impress, those on the right (below) delight the eye with their restrained use of Classical orders and sensitive detailing.

Late Anglo-Malay Bungalows

The Anglo-Malay bungalow proved to be remarkably adaptable to a variety of forms. By the beginning of the thirties, one begins to see evidence of early Modernist influences manifest themselves in simpler lines and less ornate decorative details. Verandahs also became very much reduced in extent around this time as did the windows. Generally, these later bungalows were much more European in flavour and conception. This was no doubt a reflection of the times — the interwar years saw a significant increase in the numbers of British and other Europeans resident in Singapore who brought with them the tastes and prejudices of the suburbs they had left behind. The main living floor, however, continued to be raised up on piers as of old; it was not until after the Second World War that it dropped down to ground level.

▼ Typical postwar bungalow, Braddell Heights.

By the 1950s, the Singapore bungalow had more or less shed all its Anglo-Indian features, its louvred shutters and broad eaves aside.

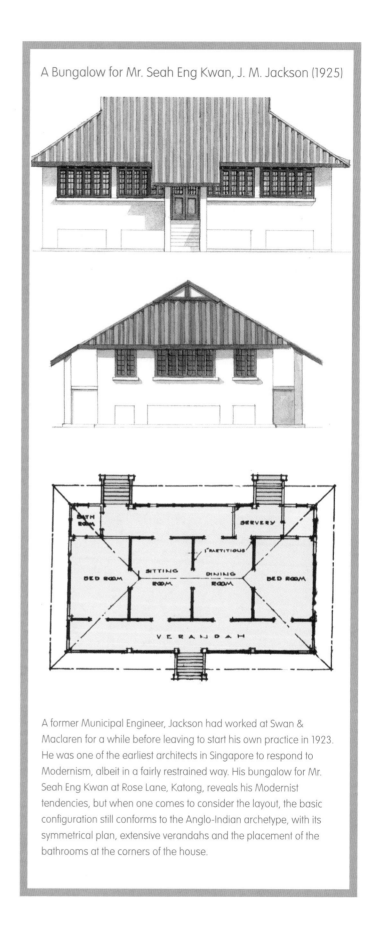

A Bungalow for Mr. Seah Eng Kwan, J. M. Jackson (1925)

A former Municipal Engineer, Jackson had worked at Swan & Maclaren for a while before leaving to start his own practice in 1923. He was one of the earliest architects in Singapore to respond to Modernism, albeit in a fairly restrained way. His bungalow for Mr. Seah Eng Kwan at Rose Lane, Katong, reveals his Modernist tendencies, but when one comes to consider the layout, the basic configuration still conforms to the Anglo-Indian archetype, with its symmetrical plan, extensive verandahs and the placement of the bathrooms at the corners of the house.

▲ Bungalow for P. B. Purvis Esq., Bukit Tunggal Estate, Booty & Edwards (1931).

The practice of Booty & Edwards was best known for their 'Dutch-style' cottages on the Bukit Tunggal estate, off Chancery Lane. They were almost entirely European in conception and could easily have been drawn directly from the pages of contemporary architectural journals in the UK. Certainly, they had very little connection with the domestic architecture that had preceded them in colonial Singapore. A characteristic feature was a dramatic, Voyseyesque downward sweep of the roof over a exposed-brick arch framing the carport.

▼ This bungalow at Peel Road dates from the mid-1930s and manages to combine both early Modernist influences — notably the largely unornamented façade and windows tucked up under the eaves in the manner of C. F. A. Voysey — with Arts and Crafts features such as the bracketed eaves.

ARTS & CRAFTS
INFLUENCES

THE MOST IMPORTANT SINGLE INFLUENCE in the genesis of the black and white house is that of the Arts and Crafts movement. The latter had its origins in the Gothic revivalist movement of the first half of the nineteenth century and the emergence of a more general interest in vernacular architecture that accompanied it. Its two leading protagonists, William Morris and John Ruskin, advocated a return to traditional building methods and medieval standards of craftsmanship, which, they felt, were in danger of disappearing altogether with the advance of industrialisation, mass production and the materialism of the machine age. 'Truthfulness,' they insisted, should be the first principle of architecture, whereby design and decoration were intimately linked to the properties of the materials used and the tasks they were intended to perform.

◀▲ House for Mr. Ong Sam Leong, Holland Road, Williams & Steadman (1912). Tropical 'Tudorbethan': late Victorian vernacular revivalism, relocated and

Oldest Black and White House?

The oldest surviving example of a black and white house in Singapore is the single-storey bungalow, Atbara, at Gallop Road, which dates from 1898. Atbara was designed by R. A. J. Bidwell of Swan & Maclaren for a gentleman by the name of John Burkinshaw, a barrister, and one of the partners in the firm of Aitken, Donaldson & Burkinshaw. The house is remarkable on a number of accounts, not least its unusual L-shaped plan and half-timbered elevations, both of which represent a radical departure from the conventional nineteenth-century bungalow. It stands on the summit of a modest eminence and is approached by a long driveway, which curves around the outside of the building, but at a lower level to the house itself, which is situated at the top of a grassy bank. A Gothic-style carriage porch straddles the driveway with a flight of stairs leading up to the main entrance, which is at the junction of the two arms of the L-shaped plan. One wing consists entirely of bedrooms, while the other is made up of a bedroom and a dining room. The principal reception room connects the two wings of the house and is surmounted by a pyramidal jack roof.

▲ Atbara, Gallop Road, R. A. J. Bidwell (1898).

The house makes the most of its dramatic location, with the drawing room situated where the two arms of the L-shaped plan meet, thus affording superb views in two directions over the surrounding Cluny estate.

▼ The Gothic-style carriage porch, complete with medieval-style crucks and braces; apart from cathedrals, churches and other ecclesiastical architecture, the Victorian Gothic revival movement did not make much of an impact in Singapore.

Atbara is a house of curiosities. Quite apart from its unusual L-shaped plan and distinctive carriage porch, there is a notable absence of verandahs. The drawing room came with concertina-style shutters which could be pushed back into the corners, thereby allowing uninterrupted views over the surrounding parkland of the Cluny estate, but the broad Anglo-Indian-style living verandah, at once so characteristic of the nineteenth-century Singapore house, was for some reason omitted, which may explain why in 1915 a bay-fronted verandah was added to the dining room wing.

Another striking thing about Atbara is the treatment of the elevations. The main fabric of the building comprises a load-bearing timber frame, filled in with half-brick panels or nogging. Now this building technique had been around for a long time, but what is interesting about Atbara is that we see here, apparently for the first time in Singapore, a deliberate attempt to make an architectural feature of this kind of construction technique. The timbers are

▲ Singapore Botanic Gardens (c.1890). The Botanic Gardens bordered the Cluny estate and both were landscaped in the eighteenth-century picturesque manner of Capability Brown and William Kent, with carefully-composed panoramas of 'natural' features such as trees and water.

▼ Atbara was unusual in many respects, not least because of the absence of verandahs. Instead, there is a grassy terrace in front of the bedroom wing of the house, reached by a staircase leading down from the drawing room.

▲ The Moorish, or Saracenic, basement supporting the main floor. Until recently, Atbara was the chancery of the French Embassy, but now stands in a sad state of disrepair.

▼ The Moorish staircase leading up from the driveway to the terrace; note the Islamic motif etched into the stucco of the newel post and the 'onion' top-knot on top.

simply deployed at regular intervals to form a rectangular grid, but whereas normally they would have been plastered over when the external walls received their rendering, in this instance they have been left exposed, creating the distinctive 'black and white' effect of timber framework and rendered panelling which was to become a key defining feature of the black and white house.

Perhaps the most curious feature of Atbara, though, is the basement. The main floor of the house is raised on masonry piers in the typical Anglo-Malay manner, but interestingly they are in the round and are linked by trefoil arches, a highly unusual detail in the architectural record for Singapore. Lee Kip Lin, in *The Singapore House*, identifies the basement as being Gothic-inspired — "the arches are English decorated while the round piers are of Norman proportions." This makes perfectly good sense, given the Gothic-style carriage porch and quasi-medieval half-timbered facades, but on closer inspection, the slight return of the trefoil arches, where the base of the arch meets the capital of the column, is actually much more reminiscent of Moorish architecture than Gothic, calling to mind of the architecture of Caliphate Spain.

This seemingly preposterous assertion is not as far-fetched as it may sound. Prior to his coming to Singapore, Bidwell had been with the Public Works Department in Kuala Lumpur where he had worked on the celebrated Government Secretariat, today's Sultan Abdul Samad Building (completed 1896). The first plans for the Secretariat were drawn up by Bidwell under the supervision of A. C. Norman, the State Architect, and were Classical in manner — the preferred style for government buildings in the colonies. State Engineer and PWD Director, C. E. Spooner, approved of the general layout, but felt that a more 'Oriental' style would befit the building's purpose and asked Norman to reconsider his original design. Although Norman is ostensibly credited with the remarkable 'Moorish' or Indo-Saracenic Gothic style that was subsequently adopted, most sources agree that it was probably Bidwell who was responsible for the new elevations. Not long afterwards, Bidwell moved to Singapore to join Swan & Maclaren. That was in 1895; three years later he designed Atbara.

The Moorish connection becomes all the more credible if one takes a look at the detailing of the external staircase leading up from the driveway to the terrace. Here one clearly sees a Moorish decorative motif excised into the stuccoed rendering of the newel post. What is more, the top of the post is surmounted by an onion-shaped 'top-knot', which recalls the Saracenic domes of Government Secretariat in Kuala Lumpur; the latter feature is repeated at intervals along the balustrading of the terrace.

A Mixed Marriage?

The mix of Moorish and Gothic influences at Atbara is highly unusual to say the least, but interestingly, Bidwell's time in Kuala Lumpur may have played a significant part in this. The fact is that Bidwell, while he was working on the Government Secretariat building, would have seen facing him across the Padang — the open green space at the very centre of Kuala Lumpur which serves as parade ground, cricket pitch, and hockey field — the celebrated Selangor Club, or 'Spotted Dog' (1890). The latter has been rebuilt, restored and otherwise transformed several times over, but is still today considered to be one of the finest examples of late-Victorian Tudor-style architecture in South East Asia. Is it not too fanciful to suggest, then, that Atbara, with its curious combination of half-timbered walls and Moorish basement, represents nothing less than a mixed marriage of architectural styles from opposite sides of the Padang in Kuala Lumpur?

▶ The Selangor Club, Kuala Lumpur (1890).

Designed by Public Works Department architect, A. C. Norman, it replaced an earlier *atap* structure on the site, which had served as a clubhouse since 1884. The new building was a two-storey affair with a tiled floor, which was raised a little above ground level since the surrounding area was prone to flooding. The basic plan was modelled on the Anglo-Indian bungalow, with a verandah running the entire length of the Padang elevation. The half-timbered elevations, on the other hand, represent perhaps the earliest example of the late-Victorian 'Tudorbethan' revival in South East Asia.

▲ The front elevation of Atbara (with the staircase leading up from the carriage porch omitted). Note the curious absence of verandahs — balconies at the back of the house provide access to the bedrooms but no more than that. Admittedly, the living room had rows of louvred windows on two sides, which could be folded back on themselves like an accordion, thereby opening up the room to the splendid views over the surrounding, park-like landscape. Even so, the house is much more enclosed than the typical Anglo-Malay bungalow of that period. In 1915 a bay-fronted verandah was added to the dining room wing, but this is still a pretty poky affair and does little more than provide an alternative means of access to the dining room and the bedroom beyond.

Kuala Lumpur - The Selangor Club

Atbara and the Red House

Atbara

The Red House

At first sight there seems little to connect Bidwell's Atbara and the Red House, designed by Philip Webb for his friend and leading Arts and Crafts luminary, William Morris. The latter is a two-storey affair with red-brick elevations, Gothic detailing and a slate roof, while Atbara is a single-storey, half-timbered bungalow, elevated on Moorish brick piers with a shingle roof (originally). However, if one turns to their respective floor plans and internal arrangement of rooms, one sees that both buildings have the same basic configuration. For the Red House, Webb favoured an L-shaped plan with the principal rooms arranged end to end, connected by a corridor running along the inside of the 'L', and precisely the same layout was employed by Bidwell at Atbara, except that in this instance a narrow verandah takes the place of Webb's connecting corridors. Similarly, the positioning of the main entrance and the location of the drawing room at the point where the two wings meet, is again exactly the same in both houses. Moreover, Atbara's distinctive Gothic-style carriage porch also points a finger in the direction of the Red House, whose entrance is similarly accented by an impressive Gothic arch — one should note here that Bidwell was for the most part Classically oriented (*viz*. his elegant façade for Raffles) and hardly ever featured Gothic elements in his work, the turret-like prospect tower he used for the Teutonia Club (today's Goodwood Park Hotel) and one or two other early commissions aside.

These correspondences between the two houses I believe to be more than simply coincidence. In its day, the Red House — arguably "the most remarkable British house of the nineteenth century" — was such a celebrated example of modern English architecture that a man of Bidwell's background and education could scarcely fail to have been on anything but the most intimate terms with its basic plan and essential features. This leaves little doubt in my mind that Bidwell's apparent 'borrowing' from Philip Webb's original design was quite deliberate on his part. Which is not to say that Bidwell was a mere copyist — Atbara is a distinctive building in its own right. More likely, he saw himself as responding to the challenge of adapting contemporary English domestic architecture to a tropical setting.

◀ Plan of Atbara, plus ground floor plan and front elevation of the Red House. Apart from a general congruence in terms of the L-shaped plan and internal arrangement of rooms, one should also note the dramatic Gothic-style entrance porch of the Red House, which finds its counterpart in the medieval carriage porch at Atbara.

The Plantation House

Sometimes referred to as the 'Plantation House' because it once stood at the centre of pepper plantation, No. 6 Russells Road on the Alexandra Park estate has little connection with the typical plantation houses of the mid-nineteenth century, being relatively small and compact, and composed around an L-shaped plan. Indeed, in this last respect, No. 6 more closely resembles John Burkinshaw's bungalow, Atbara, at Cluny Road. Like Atbara, the walls are timber-framed with brick in-fill and the main floor of the house is raised off the ground on brick piers, though in this instance the interval is spanned by robust timber beams rather than masonry arches. The main entrance is at one end of a verandah that runs the full length of the front elevation. It comprises a projecting porch at ground level with a roof supported by Gothic-style, arched braces, or crucks, a feature that is again reminiscent of the carriage porch at Atbara, though the detailing is not quite so elaborate here.

There is no record of the building in the architectural archives, but it seems from land surveys that the house was already in existence by 1905, which would make it contemporaneous with the career of Regent Alfred John Bidwell who designed Atbara in 1898. Given the similarities of the two houses, notably their L-shaped plan and Gothic entrance porches, as well as the general quality of the design work, it seems likely that Bidwell was also responsible for No. 6.

▶ No 6 Russells Road, Alexandra Park, (c.1900).
The Gothic entrance porch, with steps leading to the verandah at the front of the house.

▼ Watercolour illustration of Russells Road by Derek Corke (1996).

A flight of stairs leads up from the entrance porch to the verandah, which is long and broad and has a staircase at the far end leading down into the garden. At this point the verandah is extended outwards slightly to create a kind of cantilevered belvedere, or gazebo, where, one imagines, the original owner might have sat and gazed out across his property of an afternoon. As in the case of the entrance porch, the posts supporting the roof here are braced in a quasi-medieval fashion.

The interior of the house is notable for the extensive use of open latticework, which is incorporated into the doors and walls leading from the main verandah into the principal reception room and other parts of the house. The uppermost portion of the internal partitions of the house has also been left open, save for a loose grid of vertical and horizontal bars. Together, these features not only encourage a good circulation of air through the interior of the building, but also make for a pleasing play of light and shadow.

◀ Front verandah looking towards the entrance. The floors of the verandahs are laid with clay tiles — for the most part plain, though with a decorative border running around the margins. Inspection from below reveals that the weight of this ceramic floor is actually supported by steel joists.

▼ Gothic detailing of the belvedere.

▲ No/ 6 Russells Road: the staircase at the garden end of the front verandah (top); lattice-work and masonry piers (bottom).

The Plantation House is notable for its careful consideration of details, hinting at the likely involvement of someone with a professional architectural background such as Bidwell.

◀ Communicating verandah leading to the master bedroom.

Victorian 'Tudorbethan'

The so-called 'Tudorbethan' revival of the 1880s — a mixture of Tudor, Elizabethan and Jacobean architectural styles — reflected the spirit of Romanticism which pervaded so much of Victorian architecture, especially in the latter half of the Queen's long reign. It was characterised by half-timbered, black and white façades, steeply pitched roofs with gable ends and sculpted bargeboards, and tall brick-built chimneys. The Liverpool and Chester practice of Grayson & Ould, which specialised in Tudoresque, timber-framed villas and country houses for parvenu industrialists of the northwest, exemplifies the style, with Edward Ould's magnificent Wightwick Manor (1887–1888) being just about as good as it can get. Sometimes described, somewhat disparagingly perhaps, as mock Tudor (the label has a rather pejorative whiff about it), this was actually a fine and sensible reworking of quintessential English architectural themes, a response to Pugin and Ruskin's celebration of traditional values that could be adapted to a variety of social and economic settings. Transported to Singapore, it was a major influence on the genesis of the black and white house around the turn of the century.

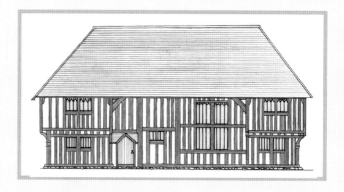

▲ Yardhurst, Great Chart, Kent; late-medieval/early Tudor great hall.

▼ Wightwick Manor, Edward Ould (1887–1888, 1893).

Edward Ould, together with his partner, George Grayson, played a leading role in the revival of Tudoresque, half-timbered architecture in the northwest of England in the last quarter of the nineteenth century. Their clients were mainly nouveau riche industrialists who aspired to the ranks of the landed gentry and Edward Ould was the man to provide them with what they wanted when it came to setting themselves up with a suitable place in the country.

R. A. J. Bidwell

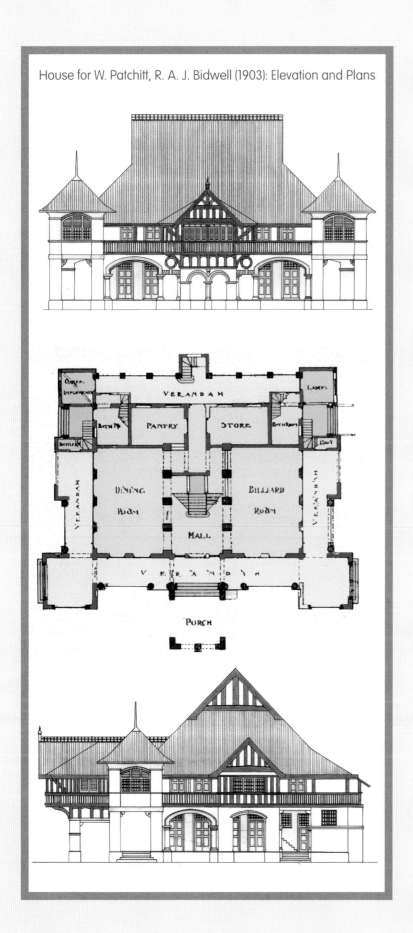

The year 1903 marks the point at which the 'black and white story' really begins, with a magnificent house for W. Patchitt at Cluny Road. Again designed by R. A. J. Bidwell at Swan & Maclaren, this building established the basic formula for the early black and white house, namely a half-timbered mock-Tudor upper storey built over a Classically detailed masonry ground floor. The house is further distinguished by a huge soaring roof and two square corner towers at either end of the front elevation, which gives the house a Jacobean touch. Internally, the plan follows the typical nineteenth-century pattern, with the rooms symmetrically arranged about a central axis and the main living area located on the first floor. A broad verandah connects the two corner towers and extends out over the centrally-placed *porte cochère* in the usual fashion. What is especially significant about this building is the detailing of the half-timbered upper floor, where the pattern of timbers is clearly modelled on fifteenth- and sixteenth-century sources. Moreover, the verandah over the *porte cochère* is extended outwards on all sides, by means of cantilevered floor joists supported from below by brackets, in the manner of a medieval jetty. Here Bidwell's Tudorbethan credentials are quite clearly demonstrated for all to see.

Not only was Bidwell blessed with considerable talent, but he was also something of a rare fish in Singapore at the turn of the century — a professionally qualified architect. A man who had been placed on the honours list of the Architectural Association of London for design, and at one time joint secretary of this prestigious organisation, Bidwell would have been well-versed with the most recent architectural trends back in London prior to his departure for the East in the early 1890s. This would have included the work of Richard Norman Shaw, pioneer of the so-called Old English style back in the 1860s, and other luminaries of the Victorian revivalist movement. We have also mentioned Bidwell's sojourn with the PWD in Kuala Lumpur and the influence that this may have had in relation to Atbara. Five years later, with his house for Mr. Patchitt, we see the mature realisation of this fruitful idea. Bidwell was without doubt the leading architect of his day in Singapore; arguably, he was also the man who was principally responsible for the genesis of the black and white house.

Tropical Mock Tudor

In its essentials, the early black and white house can be seen as the coming together of two architectural traditions. On the one hand, we have the late-nineteenth-century colonial house, with its shady verandahs, broad eaves and Classically detailed elevations. And on the other, there is the mock Tudor villa or country house of late-Victorian England, with its half-timbered façades, fretted bargeboards and decorative woodwork. There are other influences too, among them local Malay references, as well as a touch of Queen Anne revival, and a pinch of Strawberry Hill 'Gothick'. But at its core the black and white Singapore house is mock Tudor in a tropical frock. And it worked very well. The archetypal black and white house, built on either side of the First World War, comprised a solid, Classically-inspired basement floor, brick-built and ennobled by Doric or Tuscan columns, with a much lighter half-timbered upper storey. This 'Jacobethan' mix of Classical and vernacular themes was very in the style of Richard Norman Shaw, Britain's premier architect from the 1860s through to the turn of the century. Reinvented in Singapore by the likes of Bidwell and his peers it produced an elegant, if slightly whimsical, style of domestic architecture, which was easy to build, relatively inexpensive in terms of materials, and at the same time represented a sensible and environmentally-sound response to the demands of designing for an equatorial monsoon climate.

▶ Mock Tudor makeover of Woodside, Williams & Draper (1906).

Although the practice of Williams & Draper (later Williams, Draper & Steadman) was relatively short-lived — from 1906 to 1913 or thereabouts — they produced some of the finest tropical mock Tudor houses of the black and white era. Charles Williams and William Draper were former government architects who had gone into private practice on their own. Their first commission was for the prominent Singapore barrister Rowland Allen and comprised an extension and re-styling of his existing residence, Woodside, in Tanglin. At Woodside they established the essential elements of their style and no doubt the commission contributed greatly to the subsequent success of the practice. Sadly, there is but one example of their work still extant — a house for business magnate and early property developer, Ong Sam Leong, off Holland Road (see pp, 22-23) — and this is in a semi-ruinous condition.

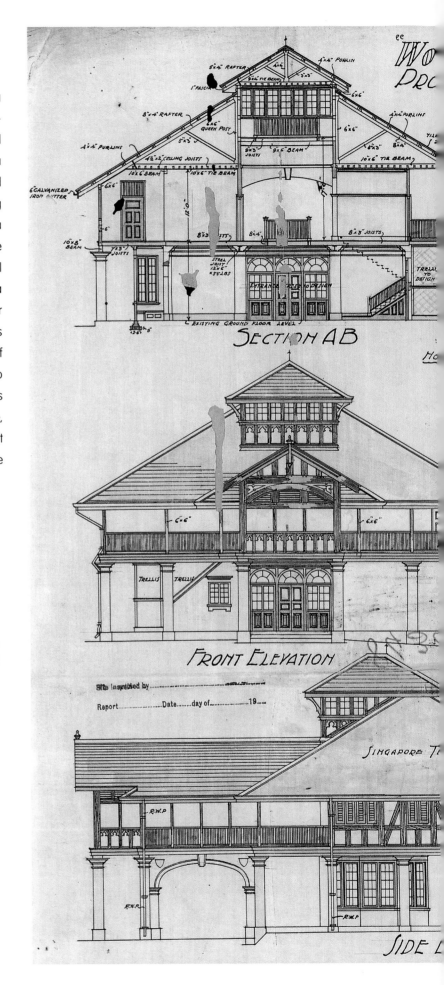

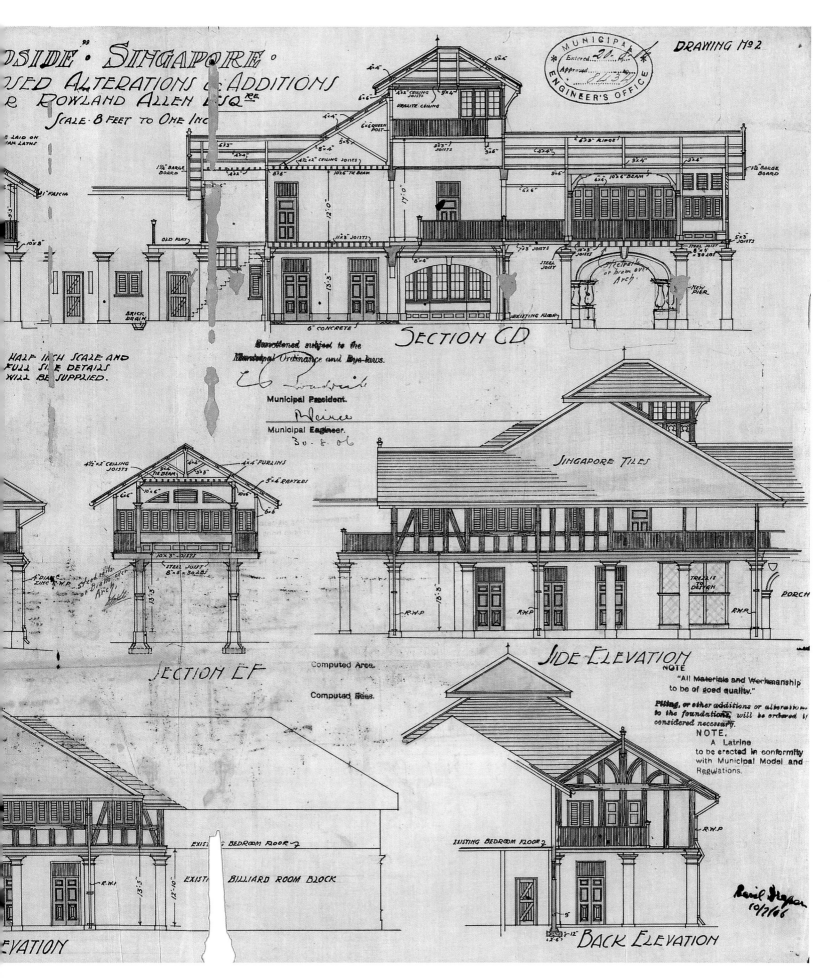

DRAWING N.º 2

...DSIDE · SINGAPORE ·
...UED ALTERATIONS & ADDITIONS
...R. ROWLAND ALLEN ESQ.ᴿᴱ
SCALE · 8 FEET TO ONE INCH

SECTION CD

HALF INCH SCALE AND
FULL SIZE DETAILS
WILL BE SUPPLIED.

Sanctioned subject to the
Municipal Ordinance and Bye-laws.

Municipal President.

Municipal Engineer.
30.8.06

SECTION EF

SINGAPORE TILES

SIDE ELEVATION

Computed Area.

Computed Fees.

NOTE
"All Materials and Workmanship
to be of good quality."

Piling, or other additions or alterations
to the foundations, will be ordered if
considered necessary.

NOTE.
A Latrine
to be erected in conformity
with Municipal Model and
Regulations.

EXISTING BEDROOM FLOOR

EXISTING BILLIARD ROOM BLOCK

EXISTING BEDROOM FLOOR

BACK ELEVATION

...EVATION

39

The sad fact is that the best black and white houses built are no longer around. They were private commissions, designed by the likes of Bidwell, Williams and Draper, and the Scots architect, David McLeod Craik, who was another former Municipality man who left the employ of the government to venture into private practice, initially on his own and later with Swan & Maclaren. These privately-owned houses were passed down from one generation to another, or else were sold on to someone else, until the value of land in Singapore reached such heights that it was no longer realistic to maintain such extravagant homes when they could be flogged off to a property developer for a truly astronomical sum. The vast majority of black and white houses that remain today have survived the passage of time because they formerly belonged to the British government — they were built by the Public Works Department, or PWD as it was better known, to provide accommodation for civil servants in the colonial administration. When independence came in 1963 they were passed on to the new Singaporean government who have kept and maintained them to this day. Some of them are very fine and imposing houses in their own right, but it would be nice if something like Bidwell's house for Mr. Patchitt, or Rowland Allen's Woodside, was still standing. As it is, they survive only on paper, secreted away in the stacks of the National Archives of Singapore, and more's the pity.

▶ The Public Works Department was one of the leading exponents of the black and white style of architecture both before and after the First World War. The houses on the Malcolm Road estate were built in the mid-twenties to provide accommodation for mid-level administrators in the Malayan Civil Service.

Stockbroker Tudor

The Public Works Department adopted the black and white formula as their house style before the First World War (*see next chapter*). By the time these houses at Stevens Road were built in the mid-1930s or thereabouts, the tropical mock Tudor idiom was beginning to wear a little and something of the originality and inventiveness of the earlier PWD houses around the corner at Goodwood Hill and Nassim Road had been lost.

At the same time, these newer houses reflect a move away from a leisurely nineteenth-century lifestyle, lived largely on open verandahs and characterised by an abundance of servants, to one that was more inward-looking and austere. Often the ground floor verandah was 'lost' altogether to be replaced by walls and windows, and although the first-floor sitting room, projecting out over the *porte cochère*, continued to be a popular formula, the latter tended to be more closed-in than before. The trend now was increasingly towards the character of the contemporary English house. These were solid middle-class homes for solid middle-class civil servants and were not that dissimilar from hundreds of new houses built between the wars on the outer fringes of London for affluent professionals in the so-called 'stockbroker belt'. The feel here was more suburban than tropical or 'colonial', which no doubt reflected the mood or disposition of the growing number of middle-class Britons who came to Singapore in the interwar years.

◀▼ PWD houses at Stevens Road (mid-1930s).

These later black and white houses reflect a move towards the adoption of a more European lifestyle than was previously the case — more stockbroker Tudor than tropical Tudorbethan.

PLANTATION HOUSE STYLE

THE EARLIEST PURPOSE-BUILT ACCOMMODATION for civi
servants seems to have been the estates at Goodwood Hill
Nassim Road and Seton Close, which went up around 1910
The government architects who designed these houses fo
the officers in Singapore's burgeoning colonial administratior
were clearly influenced by the new black and white style which
was just reaching the height of fashion at this time. However
it is equally evident that these early black and white houses
from the drawing boards of the Public Works Department were
also inspired by the so-called plantation houses of the mid-
nineteenth century — large country mansions, foursquare ir
plan, with broad eaves and deep verandahs on all sides. This
kind of anachronism seems to have been quite conscious or
the part of the PWD architects; the plantation house formula
was at once economical to build, well-suited to the climate
and in the right hands could be made to look quite
distinguished at relatively little extra cost — a brace of Classica
columns would probably suffice. Redrawn to more modes
dimensions by the architectural staff of the PWD, the plantatior
house proved equally well suited to providing suitably
impressive, yet reasonably economical, housing for colonia
civil servants in the years before the First World War.

◀ Public Works Department bungalow, Nassim Road (c.1910).

The basic form of the early PWD houses derives from the plantation houses of the mid
nineteenth century, augmented by contemporary black and white stylings.

Government Housing

The Public Works Department, or PWD as it was usually known, was an ubiquitous feature of British government during the colonial era and the architectural legacy of its collective output can still be found today in just about every corner of the former British Empire. The PWD was primarily responsible for infrastructure — roads, bridges, irrigation works, reservoirs and the like — but its brief also included the provision of accommodation for Government servants. A need for the latter was especially felt in the early years of the twentieth century as Singapore's colonial administration went through one of its periodic growth spurts in order to keep pace with the Settlement's rapidly expanding town and population.

The earliest black and white houses built by the PWD seem to have been those on Goodwood Hill, together with those in nearby Nassim Road and Seton Close. They clearly all belong to the same basic type with their symmetrical plan, two-storey elevations and projecting *porte cochère* supported by paired Tuscan columns, and are of a similar vintage, though there are differences in size and detailing. The general consensus is that they were built around 1910. Unfortunately one cannot be more precise than this, the PWD's records for this period having been lost or at least misplaced. (The PWD, being a government department, did not have to submit their working drawings to the Municipality for planning permission and kept their own records separately from those submitted by the private sector.)

Inevitably, the bureaucratic mindset that ordained the building of accommodation for civil servants required certain conformities in terms of style, materials and economy. On the one hand, these houses had to reflect British prestige in a colonial environment, yet, at the same time, they had to answer to the scrutiny of the Whitehall accountant. Obviously, there could be no extravagant expenditure on expensive or exotic materials, so the architects who designed these buildings had to make do with what was to hand, namely locally-made bricks, Chinese tiles and, above all, timber — tropical hard- and softwoods, which in those days were cheap and easy to obtain. In this respect, there was a certain expediency about the PWD house.

 No. 48 Nassim Road (c. 1910).

The Nassim Road houses, together with those at Seton Close and Goodwood Hill, were the earliest to be built for government servants by the Public Works Department in the period leading up to the First World War.

Nineteenth-Century Influences

The earliest black and white houses from the drawing boards of the PWD were clearly influenced by the new black and white style pioneered by R. A. J. Bidwell and his contemporaries around the turn of the century. At the same time, though, these early PWD houses also looked back fifty years to the plantation villas of the mid-nineteenth century. The latter evolved in the 1840s as rising property prices near the centre of town precipitated a move to the country. This coincided with a brief, but passionate enthusiasm for growing nutmeg as a commercial crop on the part of the European community. It didn't last long — a blight in 1862, "resembling leprosy in the human being", wiped out most of the island's nutmeg plantations and brought about an end to Singapore as a centre of commercial agriculture. However, in the meantime, this period saw the emergence of a new architectural style — one that was entirely homegrown — namely that of the plantation house, which, as the name suggests, was usually the focus of an agricultural estate, worked by cheap coolie labour.

The archetypal plantation house was a two-storey building, rectangular in plan, with enclosed verandahs on the upper floor and a centrally-placed porch or *porte cochère* at the front. In this respect, they followed the Palladian

▼ Two plantation houses from the 1860s, foursquare in plan with the main living floor raised one storey. Typical features represented here include a pyramidal roof of *atap* thatch (below), a projecting *porte cochère* and broad eaves. Note the timber columns supporting the outer margins of the eaves for the bottom house. This was a characteristic feature of the time — the greatly extended eaves not only kept off the rain but also prevented the fierce tropic sun from reaching the inner core of the house during the hottest part of the day.

The Evolution of the Plantation-style House (1870–1902)

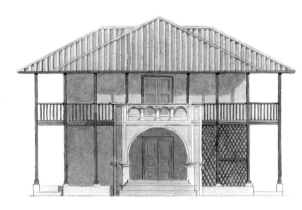

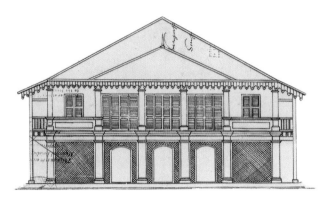

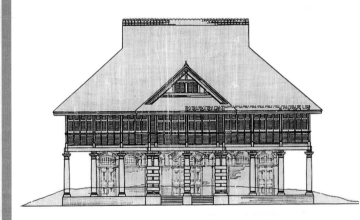

• Bellevue Cottage, Oxley Estate (1870).
• House for J. F. Nicholson, Serangoon Road (1891)
• House for sub-manager of the Hongkong & Shanghai Bank, Mount Echo (1902).
The latter was designed by R. A. J. Bidwell of Swan & Maclaren and clearly
prefigures the early black and white houses of the pre-First World War era,
while at the same time looking back fifty years to the classic plantation houses
of the mid-nineteenth century.

precedent established by Coleman down on the Esplanade; in other respects, however, they differed quite considerably.

To begin with, the ground floor was for the most part left open, though a portion might be enclosed to provide storage space and offices for the running of the estate. In the absence of load-bearing walls at ground level, the floor above was supported on brick piers and reached by a staircase of wood, which was typically situated to one side of the *porte cochère*. This upper storey consisted of large rooms, with high ceilings, arranged on a symmetrical plan, again along the lines of the Coleman model: two centrally-placed reception rooms with bedrooms on either side. There were deep verandahs, often running right round the entire upper storey, which also extended over the *porte cochère*. These were hung with rattan chics which could be lowered during the middle of the day to reduce the glare and keep the core of the house protected from the heat of the sun. In the late afternoon or early evening, they were raised again to take advantage of the ambient breezes. The high ceilings also helped to keep the rooms cool and there were *punkas* to stir the air within on the stillest of days. The upper storey was built mostly of wood, which helped to keep the building cool; often the main load-bearing timber frame was filled in with half-brick panels or nogging, a construction technique which prefigured that of the half-timbered black and white houses by some fifty years. Lastly, the steeply-pitched roof, which might be either hipped or pyramidal, was often extended much further from the external walls of the house than had hitherto been seen in Singapore, the outer margins of the eaves being supported by a row of columns or timber posts — Burkhill House in the Botanic Gardens provides a good surviving example of the latter feature.

The naturalist and ethnologist, Dr. Andreas Jagor, who visited Singapore in the 1860s, tells us that the basic design principle underlying these estate houses is "to surround the rooms in use with air on all sides and let it blow through, and to protect them from the burning sun." According to Dr. Jagor, these country houses "were the most pleasant and suited to their purpose that I have known in hot countries."

No. 3 Goodwood Hill

Number 3 Goodwood Hill is the oldest of the surviving pre-First World War PWD houses. According to former Government Architect, K. A. Brundle, the house was built around 1900 as accommodation for senior officers in the Malayan Civil Service. This information comes from Brundle's essay on 'P.W.D. Housing', which appeared in a 1952 issue of the *Quarterly Journal of the Institute of Architects of Malaya* and it seems that the PWD's prewar archives were still extant at the time, for he was able to reproduce both the plans and elevations for No. 3. An area map from 1903 confirms that No. 3 was in existence by then, though the rest of the houses on Goodwood Hill had yet to be built.

The house stands on sloping ground which falls away at the rear, and for this reason the building was placed on a brick base or stereobate. The plan is symmetrical in the style of the nineteenth century, with continuous verandahs running round three sides of the houses on both floors. The wooden verandah to the upper floor is carried by slender timber columns which continue through to support the eaves in the plantation-house manner. The ground floor is brick-built, while the upper storey is largely in timber, the whole being surmounted by a two-tiered roof, completed by 'Gothick' finials. It is a magnificent house, though, sadly, refurbishment and 'upgrading' in recent years had meant that many original features have been lost.

▶ The first of the houses for senior civil servants to be built on the Goodwood Hill estate around the turn of the century, No. 3 sees a return to the plantation-style houses of the mid-nineteenth century, with its symmetrical plan, verandahs on all sides, and a largely timber upper storey.

◣ *Porte cochère* and entrance.

▼ No.3 Goodwood Hill: front elevation and first floor plan.

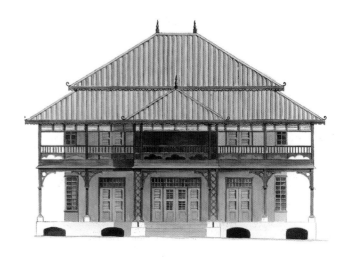

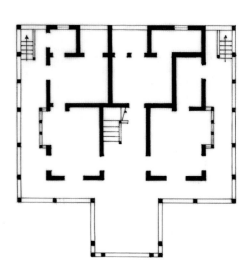

◀▲ Side elevation of No. 3 Goodwood Hill, plus ground floor and upper storey verandahs. The important thing to note here is the relationship between the central core of the building and the verandahs running round the sides. The latter function much like a sunshade, protecting the innermost recesses of the house from the heat and glare of direct sunlight.

No. 7 Goodwood Hill

Number 3 aside, all the other black and white houses on Goodwood Hill would seem to be of a similar vintage with the exception of some much later bungalows from the 1950s which were built in the gardens of the earlier houses. The general consensus is that these early PWD houses were built around 1910, though as I have indicated, this date cannot be confirmed owing to the records having been lost.

Number 7 represents the standard type. The plan is symmetrical, with a forward-projecting *porte cochère* and verandahs on all sides. The ground floor is brick-built and ennobled by Doric or Tuscan columns, which support the much lighter, half-timbered upper storey — the black and white element of the house. The ground floor consists of a central hall with a reception room to one side, and a dining room, with a scullery, or servery, attached, on the other; the main staircase is centrally placed. Upstairs, the main living area comprises a spacious, open-sided verandah, extending out over the *porte cochère*, or porch, as it was by then becoming more commonly known, with the bedrooms placed on either side. This internal arrangement of rooms on the upper storey, or *piano nobile*, can of course be traced back, via the plantation house, to the days of George Coleman and his tropical Palladian villas of the 1840s.

▶ No. 7 Goodwood Hill, Goodwood Hill (c. 1910).
A recent photograph of the house still wearing its original roof of Chinese tiles. Sadly this has been replaced since the photographs for this book were taken.

▼ Nineteenth-century plantation house with a hipped roof of *atap* thatch. The basic configuration is the same as that of the PWD houses, except that in this instance the living space is entirely on the first floor.

The side verandahs upstairs, which service the bedrooms, are carried on timber columns which extend upwards to support the overhanging eaves. This is another feature which is again reminiscent of the old plantation houses of the nineteenth century. Although piped water and proper sanitation was not introduced to most outlying residential districts until after the First World War, bathrooms had, by this time, migrated to the first floor, where they were placed at either corner at the rear of the house. A back staircase and rear verandahs provided discreet access for the servants and facilitated the noisome but necessary comings and goings of the somewhat euphemistically named *tukang ayer* (lit. 'water craftsman' in Malay), whose job it was to keep the large Shanghai storage jars filled with water for bathing and to remove the contents of the *jamban* or commode. The kitchen and servants' quarters were as always at the back of the house, detached from the main part of the building as in India, but connected by a covered walkway.

◀ The side verandahs of the upper storey at No. 7 Goodwood Hill are supported by timber columns which continue through to the underside of the eaves. This is another distinctive feature borrowed from the plantation houses of half a century earlier.

▼ Rear view of the house, showing the back staircase and covered walkway connecting the main part of the house to the detached kitchen; the servants' quarters and garages were further removed from the house.

Nassim Road and Seton Close

The Nassim Road and Seton Close estates were built by the PWD around the same time as the houses on Goodwood Hill. The Nassim Road and Seton Close houses are more or less identical to each other, albeit with minor variations since these houses were individually crafted, and they stand in a junior relation to those on Goodwood Hill, in essence being a scaled-down version of the No. 7 archetype. However, in the smaller Nassim Road and Seton Close version, the staircase is located to one side, where it is boxed in by a latticework screen as in the old plantation houses of the previous century.

Architectural historian, Norman Edwards, considering the virtues of the PWD's version of the black and white house, comments: "Designed as they were by the architects of the Public Works Department, the 'black-and-white' houses were a sensible and original interpretation of the nineteenth-century plantation house in the Tudoresque black-painted half-timbering on walls of white stucco over timber lathing." He adds: "The design calibre of such houses was not merely in their visual novelty; it was in the skilful reinterpretation of the plantation villa as a form of building appropriate to the Singaporean environment." This became the basic model and forerunner for a whole series of estates for the civil service, judiciary, police and military, which today comprises the bulk of surviving black and white houses. Most of these houses were built between the wars, but it was these earlier PWD 'black and whites' at Nassim Road and Seton Close that set the precedent for the genre.

◀▼ No. 4 Seton Close (c. 1910). The *porte cochère* makes for an agreeable sitting out verandah in modern times, the more so since in most of these houses the first-floor living room has been glazed in, in order to air-condition the principal living space.

Rank and Hierarchy

The PWD houses at Goodwood Hill, Nassim Road and Seton Close were designed with the hierarchical nature of the colonial administration in mind. Often this meant no more than a difference in size — more senior grades of official got the same house as their juniors, only bigger and with an extra bedroom and bathroom attached. At the top end of the range, though, there was greater diversity. No doubt this was consciously intended to signal the elevation of senior officers and officials over the 'other ranks', but at the same time, appearances also had to be maintained in relation to other members of Singapore's European and Asian elite. In this last respect, it was recognised that senior government officials should be seen to enjoy a similar standard of living and accommodation to their counterparts in civil society and so some of these houses built by the PWD were quite imposing buildings in their own right. At Goodwood Hill, for example, Nos. 4, 6 and 10 are each one of a kind and it is no coincidence that as well as being considerably larger than the other houses on the estate, they also enjoy the best locations on the hill.

Number 10AB is probably the grandest house on Goodwood Hill and was no doubt originally intended for a senior member of the colonial judiciary — each estate was designated for a particular category or grade of civil servant and the houses on Goodwood Hill were set aside for High Court judges and their families. Even so, for all its pomp and circumstance, the house is actually quite simple in terms of its layout, the internal arrangement of rooms being little different to the houses in nearby Nassim Road and Seton Close, albeit greatly expanded in size.

Like No. 3 Goodwood Hill, the house is more or less square in plan and sits on a raised plinth or stereobate. A broad verandah runs round all four sides of the house on both floors, and, in the case of the upper storey, is extended outwards over a forward-projecting carriage porch or *porte cochère*. So far, so much the same.

 No. 10AB Goodwood Hill.

Standing tall and imposing, on rising ground, the house is a physical reminder and endorsement of the power and prestige of a senior colonial administrator.

A short flight leads up from the driveway to the front verandah, from which one passes through to a central hallway with huge, high-ceilinged, reception rooms on either side. The main staircase is centrally placed and leads upstairs to the principal living area — a broad and spacious verandah, extending out over the *porte cochère*. The latter was originally open on all sides, with bamboo chics that could be lowered or raised according to the time of day and inclination of the elements. Light and breezy, this so-called sitting verandah was arguably *the* definitive feature of the Singapore house for much of the colonial era. Unfortunately, the tendency in recent years has been to close in these spaces with glazed casement windows for the purposes of air-conditioning. Quite apart from spoiling the general appearance of the building, this measure has also tended to diminish the sense of intimacy that formerly existed between these houses and their natural surroundings — the low hum and damp chill of an air-conditioning unit is no substitute for the call of tropical birdsong or the scent of frangipani on a balmy evening breeze, one feels.

▲ The main sitting verandah of No. 10AB Goodwood Hill projects out over the *porte cochère*, a design feature which ultimately dates back to the earliest days of Singapore and the tropical Palladian villas of George Coleman. Prior to the advent of air-conditioning, this huge space would have been open on all sides to the breezes; the hilltop location would have further enhanced the natural ventilation of the house.

▶ Interior views of the ground floor reception rooms and main staircase at 10AB Goodwood Hill. In the larger houses of more senior members of the colonial administration, the downstairs reception rooms would have been used for entertaining in a formal capacity, whilst upstairs was reserved for family life.

TROPICAL EDWARDIAN

THE PWD HOUSES AT GOODWOOD HILL looked back to the plantation-style houses of the nineteenth century and in this respect were firmly anchored in Singapore's architectural past, but one can also find contemporary examples of the black and white house which were rather more 'English' in feel. The internal arrangement of rooms is like that of houses from the same period in England and their orientation is more inward looking — the expansive verandahs of the Anglo-Indian days are often much reduced in extent, becoming more like balconies, and the fenestration is similar to that of an English house from the turn of the century. Perhaps the best description of this kind of house would be 'tropical Edwardian', signalling a certain correspondence with houses of the same period in England.

◀ ▲ Jointers' Quarters, Eastern Extension Australasia & China Telegraph Co., Morse Road, R. A. J. Bidwell (1908). As at Atbara, Bidwell used an L-shaped plan, and, like Atbara, there is a noticeable absence of verandahs. There was, however, originally a sitting verandah, placed in the angle between the two wings. This can be seen in the photograph taken in the early 1920s, but has since been removed.

Inverturret, Gallop Road

R. A. J. Bidwell's house for Charles McArthur, on the Cluny estate in 1906, represents another significant departure from the archetypal three-bay Singapore house of the previous century. For Inverturret, Bidwell eschewed the Classical symmetry of the conventional Singapore house of the nineteenth century, opting instead for a more or less square plan with the internal arrangement of rooms being organised along much more organic principles in terms of circulation and usage. In this last respect, Inverturret was more like contemporary houses then being built in England. At the same time, though, it was still very much a house designed for the tropics, with its broad eaves and generous verandahs running round all four sides. Bidwell's innovative spirit and his willingness to approach each new commission from a fresh perspective were hallmarks of his career.

▲ Inverturret, garden elevation, R. A. J. Bidwell (1906).

The bay-window extension, which was such an ubiquitous feature of middle-to-late-Victorian architecture back in England, was not much see in Singapore, but makes a rare appearance here.

▶▶ Inverturret interiors: first-floor verandah (top); principal reception room viewed from the entrance hall (middle); side verandah with bay extension (bottom).

Inverturret, R. A. J. Bidwell (1906): Elevation and Plans

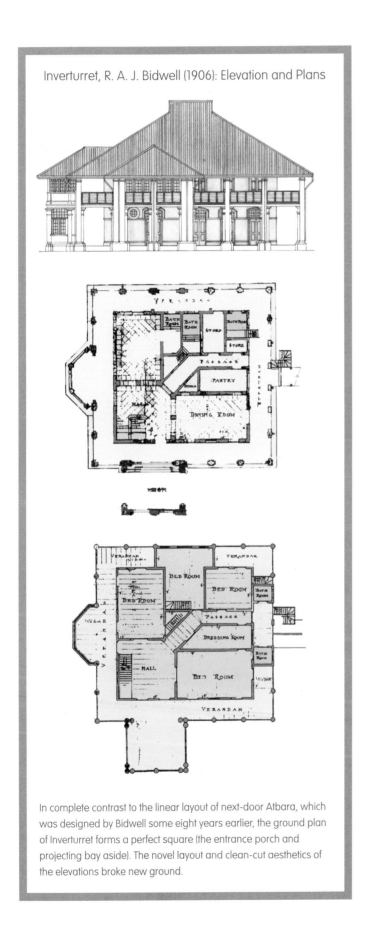

In complete contrast to the linear layout of next-door Atbara, which was designed by Bidwell some eight years earlier, the ground plan of Inverturret forms a perfect square (the entrance porch and projecting bay aside). The novel layout and clean-cut aesthetics of the elevations broke new ground.

Mohamed Namazie House

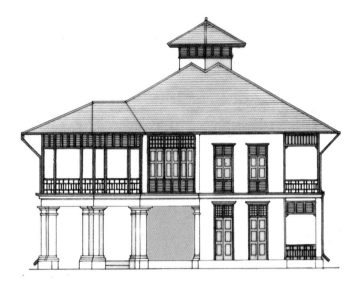

Another good example of the tropical Edwardian style is a house for Municipal Commissioner, Mohamed Namazie, on Nathan Road, designed by David McLeod Craik in 1913. A former government architect in the Municipal Engineer's office, Craik had just joined Swan & Maclaren, after some time in practice on his own, and the Namazie house was one of his first commissions for the firm. Like Inverturret, the ground plan is square, and the rooms are organised in terms of their use and patterns of circulation through the house rather than subscribing to any notion of Classical symmetry. A distinctive feature is the main entrance porch which is placed at one corner and set at an angle of 45 degrees to the main body of the house; this was quite a popular configuration at the time. A light and airy sitting verandah, with timber shutters and glazing, extends from the drawing room over the porch and each bedroom on the first floor has its own private balcony or verandah. The whole is surmounted by a pyramidal roof, topped by a lantern-like jack roof, which helps to light and provide ventilation for the centre of the house.

◀▲ House for Municipal Commissioner Mohamed Namazie, D. M. Craik (1913). Like Inverturret, the façades are clean-cut and relatively restrained in terms of detailing, giving the house a more modern, less vernacular, feel.

▼ First-floor sitting verandah, Nathan Road.
Possible Chinese influences can be discerned in the screen separating the verandah from the drawing room, but these are just as likely to have been derived from Arts and Crafts sources as they are evidence of any local input. Although sadly neglected in recent years, the house is now being included as part of a redevelopment package for the site.

Variations on a Theme

Bidwell seems to have been the first to make use of a square plan with the *porte cochère* set at 45 degrees in his house for G. A. Kesting Esq., at Mount Alba, in 1904. He revisited the idea in a house for the Hon. Dr. D. J. Galloway at Cairnhill in 1913 — this happened to be Bidwell's last completed major work before his early death in 1918. David McLeod Craik, used a very similar layout for Municipal Commissioner Namazie's house that same year (preceding page) and returned again to the theme the following year in his house for E. S. Nathan Esq. at Chatsworth Road. The angled entrance porch continued to be a popular design feature right up until the Second World War.

▼ Lanterns and belvederes were popular features at this time: a house for Miss J. Motion, St. Thomas Walk (1900) (below); Police Inspector-General's residence, Mount Pleasant (date unknown) (bottom).

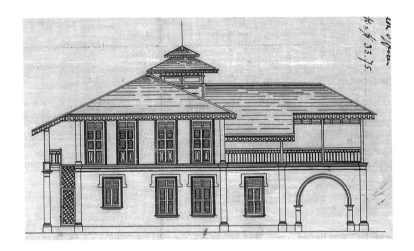

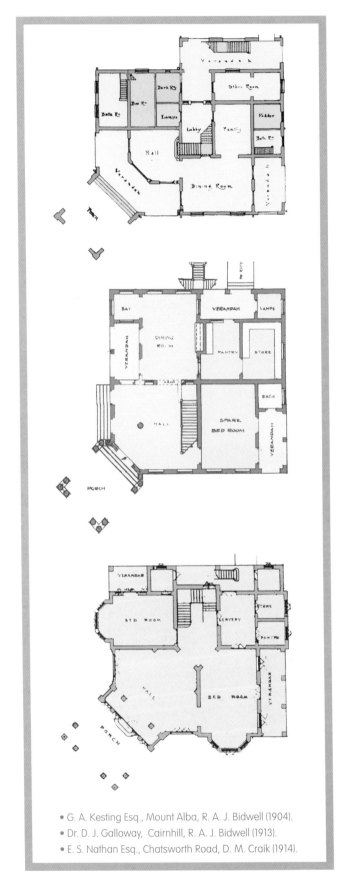

• G. A. Kesting Esq., Mount Alba, R. A. J. Bidwell (1904).
• Dr. D. J. Galloway, Cairnhill, R. A. J. Bidwell (1913).
• E. S. Nathan Esq., Chatsworth Road, D. M. Craik (1914).

Ealing on the Equator

▲ Typical bay-fronted Edwardian town house, Ealing, Middlesex. Self-proclaimed 'Queen of the Suburbs' since 1904, Ealing represented the archetypal genteel suburb of the Edwardian era — a fashionable and salubrious place to live on the western outskirts of London, at once removed from the smog of the city, yet still close enough for an easy daily commute by train.

▼ House for Dr. D. J. Galloway, Cairnhill, R. A. J. Bidwell (1913); this was to be Bidwell's last major commission before his death in 1918.

Strictly speaking, the Edwardian era only lasted from the death of Queen Victoria, in 1901, until 1910, when George V succeeded to the throne of Britain, but as an epoch it has come to represent a rather wider timeframe, extending on either side of the relatively short reign of Edward VII. In architectural terms, the Edwardian house can be seen as the culmination of an evolutionary line beginning with the Gothic revival and ending in the Arts and Crafts movement, taking in Ruskin, William Morris and Richard Norman Shaw along the way. It was a composite style, a new English vernacular, made up from a little bit of this and a little bit of that — brick façades and half-timbered gables, Gothic bargeboards and terracotta roof pieces, wooden balconies and stone lintels, tessellated tiles and stained-glass windows. Comfortable and compact, it provided the architecture for countless leafy, middle-class suburbs that were just then being built up and down the British Isles. Transplanted to Singapore and exposed to the influence of the existing colonial architecture of the Straits Settlements, it gave rise to the tropical Edwardian house, at once recognisably 'Eastern' yet at the same time wearing an ineffably English air. R. A. J. Bidwell and David McLeod Craik were the principal exponents of this new style, which no doubt reflected, in part, their own architectural training and experience prior to coming out East — the fact that both men were professionally qualified architects, was something of a novelty in Singapore at that time.

HOUSE AT CAIRN HILL:
FOR
: DR HON. D. J. GALLOWAY:

The Admiral's House

The so-called Admiral's House, splendidly situated on the Bukit Chermin promontory, looking out across the strait to Sentosa, dates from around 1915, but there is some uncertainty as to exactly whom this house was built for. Some sources suggest that it may have been for the Flag Officer Commanding the Royal Navy's China Squadron, others, for the Harbour Master of the Port of Singapore. Both are equally plausible.

As regards the first possibility, one should note that with the outbreak of the First World War in August 1914, the headquarters of the China Squadron were immediately transferred to Singapore, the island being strategically better-placed than Hong Kong in as far as the defence of Britain's imperial interests in the Far East were concerned. Alexander Still, editor of the *Straits Times*, later noted, "outside the British Isles, no naval command was more vitally important than that which had its shore quarters at Fort Canning." It was only right, then, that the Commanding Officer should have a residence built for him that was in keeping with his elevated position in the great scheme of things.

▶ The combination of Classical and vernacular elements at Bukit Chermin brings to mind the American Colonial style of New England — more George Washington than George III.

▼ The view looking across to Labrador Point. When the house was built there was a jetty at the end of the garden and the story goes that newly-arrived captains of His Majesty's Ships found it more convenient to report to their commanding officer by jumping in a cutter and coming ashore on his very doorstep, rather than making the longer journey round by road from Keppel Harbour.

The alternative possibility is that the house was erected by the Singapore Harbour Board. In 1915, the Harbour Board was halfway through a massive programme of building works to extend and refurbish Singapore's port facilities at Keppel Harbour and the Tanjong Pagar basin (see p.88). It may be that the Admiral's House was built then as a suitably impressive residence for the Harbour Master of this new, greatly improved Port of Singapore. (In this instance, one should note that immediately after the war, the hill behind the Admiral's House was developed as a residential estate for Harbour Board staff.)

▶ The grand staircase at the centre of the Admiral's House is lit from above by windows, headed by Regency-style, segmental fanlights.

▼ Suffuse with light and cooled by sea breezes, the sitting verandah offers commanding views over the western approaches to Keppel Harbour.

▲ Huge Doric columns frame the first-floor drawing room, providing a suitably grand backdrop for the reception of naval commanders, admirals of the fleet and other high-ranking officials of the empire. Classical architecture never really fell from fashion in Britain's colonial territories, where it continued to serve as an expression of British ascendency and imperial might until the very end.

Architecturally, the Admiral's House reflects a revival of Classical forms during the Edwardian era. By 1902, Richard Norman Shaw, pioneer of the Old English neo-vernacular style some forty years before, was proclaiming, "the Gothic revival, for all practical purposes, is dead." The ever-adaptable, Shaw was himself a leading protagonist in the return to Classicism, reinventing himself as the purveyor of a free neo-Classical style that combined Dutch gables, Tuscan columns and Georgian, segmentally-headed, sash windows. This came to be known as his Queen Anne style and was very much in vogue from the 1870s onwards. The Admiral's House, with its Regency fanlights and imposing portico, can be seen as a local manifestation of this neo-Georgian revival.

POSTWAR
APOTHEOSIS

THE ARCHETYPAL BLACK AND WHITE HOUSE was very much a product of the Edwardian era and those halcyon days of empire before the First World War. With the outbreak of hostilities in August 1914, house-building naturally went into something of an abeyance; otherwise, life in the Straits Settlements continued pretty much as normal and in 1918 Singapore architects simply picked up from where they had left off four years previously. This included a return to the black and white house of the prewar years and some of the finest black and white houses belong to that early postwar period. Between 1919 and 1923, over sixty tropical Tudorbethan-style houses were commissioned and built in the private sector and in terms of numbers, this period represents the high water mark of the black and white house.

◀ Eastern Extension Australasia & China Telegraph Co., Holt Road, Swan & Maclaren (1919).

The end of the First World War precipitated a boom in house-building in Singapore, with the colony's leading architectural practice, Swan & Maclaren, receiving commissions for over forty houses from more than thirty clients in the first fifteen months after the conclusion of hostilities in Europe.

The EEA&C Telegraph Co. was one of Swan & Maclaren's biggest clients in the immediate postwar era, commissioning eight houses for the company's new residential estate between Jervois Road and Nathan Road (Holt Road and Cable Road were built to provide access to the estate). Because of the nature of the site, some of the houses were set back from the driveway, requiring a covered way extending to the front door to afford visitors protection from Singapore's fierce tropic sun and torrential monsoon rain.

A Black and White Renaissance

The large numbers of black and white houses that were commissioned during the house-building boom of the immediate postwar era proved that the style was still very much in fashion, despite a four-year layoff. While mock Tudor was fast becoming a cliché in suburban England by the 1920s, in Singapore the style persisted, partly, one suspects, because it worked so well in the tropical environment. As Norman Edwards observes, in the local context, "Tudor half-timbering became much more meaningful and original."

Again it was Swan & Maclaren, Singapore's premier architectural practice, which led the way, though by this time Bidwell had left the firm in rather mysterious circumstances. Although Bidwell had been a partner since 1899 and was very much the driving force behind the firm in the first decade of the new century, around 1909 he resigned his partnership, but stayed on as a staff architect. The reasons behind this move are unclear; suffice to say, by 1912 he had left the practice altogether and was on his own.

The leading black and white man at Swan & Maclaren at the end of the First World War and immediately after, was Herbert Courtney Aitkinberry, a surveyor by training, but nonetheless very adept at turning out beautifully considered half-timbered houses in a variety of different styles. Most of the early postwar commissions received by Swan & Maclaren seem to have been by him, including a couple of houses for the Straits Trading Company which were on the drawing board before the war was even over.

▶ Eastern Extension Australasia & China Telegraph Co., Morse Road (1919). In addition to the new Cable Road estate, the EEA&C Telegraph Co. also commissioned Swan & Maclaren to design three further houses for their existing estate at Telok Blangah, two of which are still standing today.

▼ Straits Trading Co., Bushy Park, Swan & Maclaren (1918).

FRONT ELEVATION

Corporate Housing

Many of the black and white houses built by Swan & Maclaren immediately after the war were corporate commissions, intended as accommodation for expatriate staff from the major commercial houses. No doubt this was partly due to a backlog which had built up during the war, but it also reflected an upsurge in business following the conclusion of hostilities. Indeed, the immediate postwar period was something of a boom time for Singapore as the resumption of normal maritime trade brought an end to wartime shortages and created a sudden increase in demand for imported goods. More importantly, as far as long-term prospects were concerned, the First World War had proved beneficial for the Singapore rubber exchange and the local rubber industry generally, stimulating regional sales and encouraging direct shipments to the west coast of the United States, as well as to Russia and Japanese markets (previously the world's rubber trade had been almost entirely centred in London).

All of this was good news for the Singapore economy and attracted a lot of new business, among them multi-nationals like the American Firestone Tire Co. which were looking to establish a presence in the region. In 1919 Swan & Maclaren was literally inundated with corporate work. As well as Firestone, there were houses for the Oriental Telephone & Electric Co., the Eastern Extension Australasia & China Telegraph Co., Eastern United Assurance, Adamson & Gilfillan, the Borneo Company, Boustead & Co., Katz Bros., Mansfield & Co., Paterson Simons & Co., the Hongkong & Shanghai Bank and the Chartered Bank of India, Australia & China (today's Standard Chartered Bank), as well as another brace of houses for Straits Trading.

With all this work on their books, it was perhaps not surprising that Swan & Maclaren sometimes used the same design for more than one client. Not only were the houses they built for the Oriental Telephone & Electric Co., Katz Bros. and Paterson Simons in 1919 identical, but ultimately the design was derived from the Straits Trading houses at Bushy Park the preceding year (see p.78).

▶ W. H. Mansfield & Co., Sri Menanti, Swan & Maclaren (1921). Mansfield's was one of Singapore's oldest shipping agencies, the eponymous Walter Mansfield having established the firm in 1864. The pair of houses erected in 1921 on the old Sri Menanti estate (a former nutmeg plantation), exemplifies Swan & Maclaren's early postwar style.

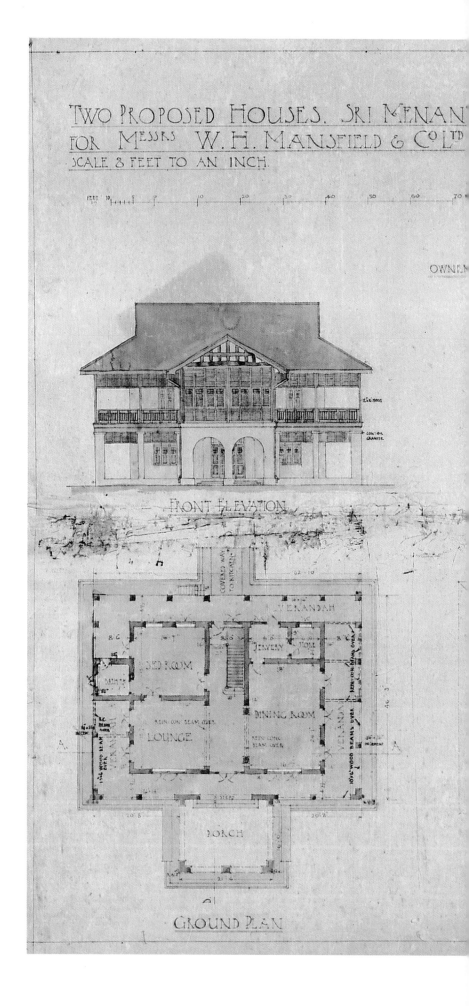

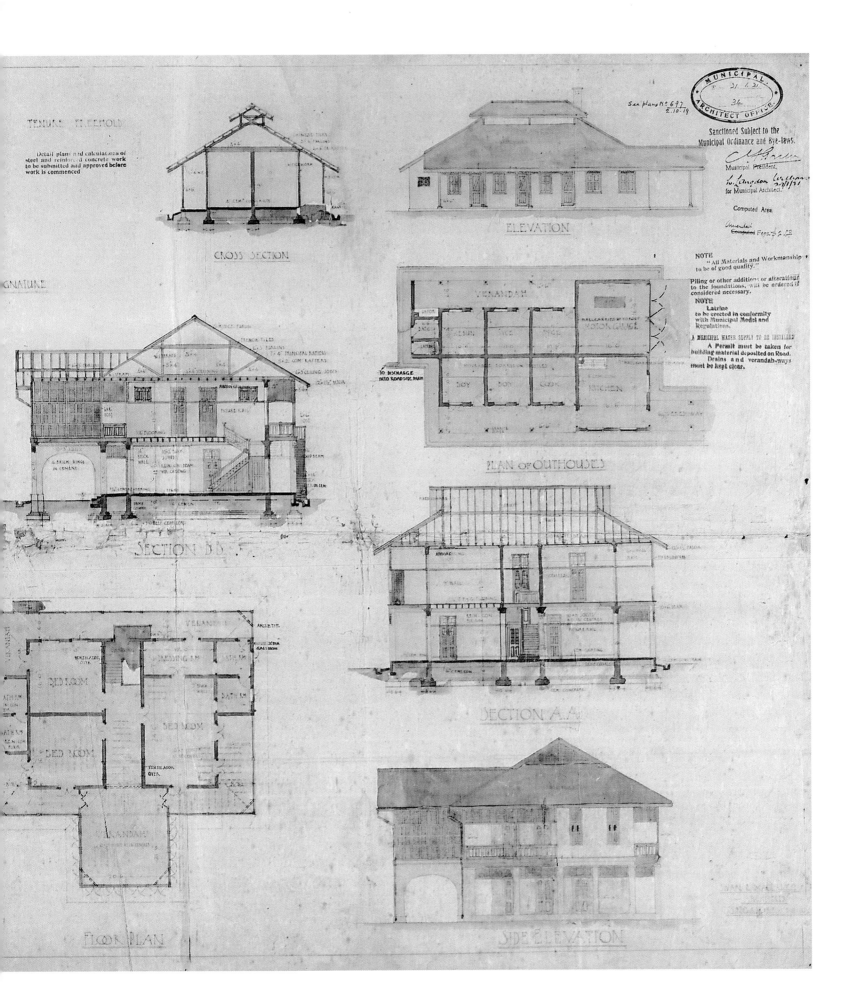

CROSS SECTION

ELEVATION

Sanctioned Subject to the
Municipal Ordinance and Bye-laws.

Municipal President.

for Municipal Architect.

Computed Area

NOTE
"All Materials and Workmanship
to be of good quality."

Piling or other additions or alterations
to the foundations, will be ordered if
considered necessary.

NOTE
Latrine
to be erected in conformity
with Municipal Model and
Regulations.

A MUNICIPAL WATER SUPPLY TO BE INSTALLED

A Permit must be taken for
building material deposited on Road.
Drains and verandah-ways
must be kept clear.

TENURE FREEHOLD

Detail plans and calculations of
steel and reinforced concrete work
to be submitted and approved before
work is commenced

SIGNATURE

SECTION BB

PLAN OF OUTHOUSES

SECTION AA

FLOOR PLAN

SIDE ELEVATION

81

Houses for the Telegraph Co.

The Eastern Extension Australasia & China Telegraph Co. was one of Swan & Maclaren's biggest clients in the immediate postwar era, with commissions for eight houses at Holt and Cable Roads in 1919, and another three in the same year at their Telok Blangah estate — Morse and Pender Roads — not to mention a bungalow off Newton Road for "the Madras staff".

Pender Road was named after Sir John Pender (1815–1896), the man who virtually single-handedly masterminded the global cable telegraphy revolution of the 1870s — his Atlantic Telegraph Company was the first to successfully connect Europe with America by submarine cable in 1865. In 1873 he amalgamated three telegraph companies — the British Indian Extension, The China Submarine and the British Australian — to form the Eastern Extension Australasia and China (EEA&C) Telegraph Company. It was this company, combined with the Eastern Telegraph Company, that formed the core of his communications network of the British Empire. With the outbreak of the First World War, the upsurge in traffic and in-operability of the Indo-European land-lines which passed through enemy territory, led to all communications with India and the Far East being transferred to the Eastern Telegraph Company. The EEA&C Telegraph Co. benefited enormously from this increase in telegraphic communication, with the company's annual receipts rising from £131,000 before the war to £950,000 in 1915 alone, more than half of which was profit. By the time the war ended, the British Empire embraced more than a quarter of the world's population and land surface, and the cable communications network which had largely been put in place by the Eastern Telegraph Company had effectively become its central nervous system. The Singapore station played a crucial role in this scheme of things, acting as the regional hub for cable services to the Far East and Australasia. As a consequence, there was a dramatic increase in expatriate staff immediately following the end of the war which was reflected in the addition of three more houses to the Telok Blangah estate as well as the building of an entirely new estate between Holt and Cable Roads.

▶ No. 3 Pender Road, Eastern Extension Australasia & China Telegraph Co., Swan & Maclaren (1919).

The house is one of the last surviving examples of the classic, tropical Tudor-style black and white house, designed by Swan & Maclaren in the immediate postwar era. There is another example, also commissioned by the EEA&C Telegraph Co., a little further up the slopes of Mount Faber at the end of Morse Road (see pp. 78-79), which incidentally was named after Samuel Morse, the inventor of cable telegraphy in the United States.

▲ Telok Blangah estate: front elevation.

◀▼ Patio and sitting verandah. Situated on the lower slopes of Mount Faber, the house, when it was first built, would have had fine uninterrupted views across to the island of Sentosa.

The Cable Road and Telok Blangah estate houses were all the same basic type — two-storey, tropical mock Tudor, with an L-shape plan. These houses, though roomy, were more compact in terms of the internal arrangement of rooms, compared with prewar houses, reflecting a new postwar austerity, with fewer servants and less lavish lifestyles. A characteristic feature of many postwar houses from the drawing boards of Swan & Maclaren is the louvred panels used as sunscreens or in place of balustrading for the verandahs — this design detail was adopted by the firm as more or less standard practice in the immediate postwar era. Another postwar innovation was the employment of diamond-shaped cement shingles in place of roof tiles. These have since been replaced by modern roofing materials at Pender Road, but the original shingles can still be seen in place on the Swan & Maclaren bungalows and mess for McAlister & Co. at Cable Road (see p. 87).

McAlister & Co., Cable Road

McAlister mess, Cable Road, Swan & Maclaren (1920). The mess is still standing; like the EEA&C Telegraph Co. houses which once stood opposite on the Holt Road estate on the other side of Cable Road, it embraces the quintessential elements of the classic postwar black and white house.

The McAlister bungalows on Cable Road are interesting because they are built on the ground in the Anglo-Indian manner, rather than being raised on piers in the Anglo-Malay style, which was unusual for the time. Although the house on stilts gradually began to fade from the scene from the 1930s onwards, it was not until after the Second World War that it disappeared altogether.

Founded in 1857, McAlister's was one of the longest-established trading houses during the colonial era. From the beginning of the twentieth century its principal business interests lay in shipping, coal and exports, and there were branches in Penang, Ipoh and Kuala Lumpur. In 1920, Swan & Maclaren were commissioned to build a mess and four bungalows for the firm on Cable Road. All the major European firms in Singapore at that time had a mess for unmarried members of staff — a place where bachelors lived and took their meals together. Early marriage was frowned upon and it was often specifically stipulated in the terms of employment that juniors would not be permitted to marry until at least one tour of duty had been completed (a tour of duty was typically of three years' duration, followed by six months' home leave).

Singapore Harbour Board

One of the biggest house-builders in the immediate postwar period was the government-run Singapore Harbour Board, or SHB as it was more familiarly known. The SHB was a corporate statutory body responsible for administering the island's port facilities and for many years was the most important public utility in Singapore. Between 1919 and 1922, the SHB embarked on an extensive house-building programme in the Telok Blangah area to provide accommodation for their rapidly growing numbers of European members of staff. New residential estates — Everton, Raeburn, Spottiswoode, Kampong Bahru and Berlayar Hill — were attractively laid out in the hilly Telok Blangah area, with the roads following the natural contours of the land and the houses placed to make the best advantage of the local topography. The houses were designed by the Harbour Board's own Estate Office and there was a wide range of basic types which varied in shape and size according to the seniority and marital status of the intended occupant. Designated 'A', 'B', 'C' and so on, right the way through to a type 'O', they were also quite varied, stylistically, ranging from updated versions of the Anglo-Malay bungalow, which were presumably intended for more junior members of staff, to quite imposing villas, which were more in the tropical Edwardian style. But of the dozens of houses that were built by the SHB in the Telok Blangah and Tanjong Pagar area just after the First World War, only a handful of the more modest bungalow types are still standing today on the slopes of Bukit Chermin and at Seah Im Road.

Singapore Harbour Board Estate Office Houses

• Type 'N', Telok Blangah Estate (1919).
• Type 'G', Spottiswoode and Raeburn Estates (1919).

▼ The magnificent Empire Dock at Tanjong Pagar, completed in 1917 as the culmination of the Singapore Harbour Board's programme to modernise and extend Singapore's port facilities which began in 1905.

Postwar PWD Houses

The boom years immediately following the end of the First World War were accompanied by a substantial increase in Government spending on the police force, education and medical services. This was partly in order to make good past deficiencies and to catch up with work that had been interrupted by the war, but it was also a reflection of the urgent need to keep up with Singapore's rapidly growing population — Chinese immigration figures in the late twenties were among the highest ever. The expansion of schools and medical facilities meant an increase in the number of Europeans who were contracted by the Government to run these services. At the same time, more civil servants were required to run the increasingly complex colonial administration and in the early-to-mid twenties, quite a large number of new houses were built to accommodate this sizeable standing army of government officials. Their occupants included police officers, senior magistrates and High Court judges, as well as medical officers and engineers, not to mention the full complement of scribes and bureaucrats down in Empress Place.

The early postwar civil service estates were mainly built to the north of Bukit Timah Road, on crown land bordering Mount Pleasant, Malcolm Road, and Chancery Lane; later they included Adam Park off Farrer Road and other more distant locations from the centre of town. The standard type of housing here was again the black and white bungalow.

▲ Singapore Improvement Trust (SIT) mess, Kay Siang Road. The SIT was a government-financed statutory body created in 1927 to improve housing for Singapore's poor in an early attempt at slum clearance. In 1960, its functions were taken over by the Housing Development Board.

▼ PWD bungalow, Malcolm Road (c.1925).

PWD Houses, Malcolm Road

Taking a look at the PWD houses on Malcolm Road, these were built around 1925 and were designated as Class III government housing. They were designed by H. A. Stallwood, ARIBA, Government Architect from 1922 to 1928. Although they are firmly in the black and white tradition of the prewar PWD houses, they also show signs of moving with the times. The Classical references that enriched the houses on Goodwood Hill, Nassim Road and Seton Close before the war have been lost, or at least pared down, and the detailing is much simpler — there are even signs of contemporary Art Deco influences.

A particularly interesting development is the use of the natural topography of the site as an integral element in the design of the house. Built on sloping ground, the basement floor is open except for the entrance hall and stairwell, and a garage to one side. The main living floor, which is all on one level, is raised on concrete piers at the front, just like the old plantation villas of the nineteenth century, but because the site rises up behind the house, the back of the building is actually at ground level. The plan is long and narrow — only one room deep — with a continuous verandah at the front and back. The rooms are symmetrically arranged around a central axis. A drawing-room cum sitting verandah occupies the centre of the bungalow and extends out over the *porte cochère*, or 'car port' as it had come to be known by this time, while the dining room is situated behind as in the archetypal Coleman-style villa. The bedrooms are placed on either side, again following the Coleman archetype, but in this instance they are strung out in a line with access via front and rear verandahs. The kitchen and servants' quarters remain detached from the main part of the house, as was the norm; they are at the back and are built on the ground, but because of the sloping site, this meant that they were actually at the same level as the rest of the house (or even slightly higher). This was not the first time that this kind of house had been seen in Singapore — there are several earlier instances of houses built on sloping sites in the architectural record which are similar in their conception. However, they were one-off commissions in the private sector and not necessarily in the black and white style. At Malcolm Road, the split-level, side-of-a-hill house becomes a distinct architectural genre in its own right.

◀ No. 39 Malcolm Road, PWD (c.1925).
The archetypal PWD bungalow of the interwar years, a long and thin, single-storey affair, built on the side of a hill, with the main living floor raised on brick or reinforced concrete piers.

▲▲▶ No. 39 Malcolm Road: entrance porch, front door and drawing room.

The ornamentation of these later PWD bungalows is altogether different from the earlier plantation-style house from before the First World War. Classical references have been done away with, while the detailing of doors and windows is at once recognisably contemporary in execution, with just the faintest hint of the celebrated Glaswegian architect, Charles Rennie Mackintosh, about them. Even the half-timbering has been given a modern makeover— no faux-medievalism here!

Mount Rosie

This former PWD bungalow at Mount Rosie belongs to the same Malcolm Road development of the mid-twenties. In this instance, one sees more clearly the evidence of Modernist influences in the detailing of the columns, which have a distinctly Art Deco feel to them. Similarly, the half-timbered upper storey is given a rationalist treatment and is less anachronistic than the earlier prewar black and white houses, which were more self-consciously Tudorbethan in their execution. Government Architect, H. A. Stallwood, who is attributed with the design of these bungalows, was also responsible for the military headquarters at Fort Canning (1918) and despite differences in scale and purpose, one can discern a basic affinity between the two types of building — both are based on a long and narrow plan, serviced by communicating verandahs front and back, which makes for good cross ventilation.

▼▶ The long, linear plan of the Malcolm Road/Mount Rosie houses was subsequently adopted as the standard PWD bungalow style of the interwar years and significant numbers can still be found at Adam Park, Kay Siang Road and other former civil services estates dating from that period. The particular house featured here has recently been restored and the unsightly lean-to garage removed.

Mount Pleasant

The leafy enclave of Mount Pleasant is where one finds some of the grandest government-built black and white houses after Goodwood Hill. They were built between the wars to provide accommodation for Police Inspectors-general and other high-ranking colonial officers — Mount Pleasant was developed in conjunction with the Police Academy at the bottom of the hill. Clearly, these houses had to be at least as big as the largest residences in Tanglin and other residential areas in the private sector in order that they might be seen to be appropriate to the dignity of their occupants. The earliest Mount Pleasant houses were based on the plantation-style prototype first introduced by the PWD at Goodwood Hill; later examples trace the trajectory of the black and white house's subsequent evolution in the years leading up to the war in the Pacific. Under the Japanese Occupation, several of these house were taken over by the Kempeitai — the dreaded Japanese military police who were responsible for many atrocities and murders during that dismal period — and many taxi drivers today will refuse a fare to Mount Pleasant after dark for fear of encountering the ghosts of their unfortunate victims.

◀▼ No. 5 Mount Pleasant Road, PWD (c.1920s).
Three quarters of a century after they were built, the houses on Mount Pleasant now enjoy a superb mature jungle setting, which is to be preserved under the Heritage Roads scheme, introduced in May 2005.

FRANK BREWER
LATE ARTS & CRAFTS

THE HEYDAY OF THE CLASSIC Swan-&-Maclaren-style postwar black and white house was relatively short-lived and by the mid-1920s, the Singapore house was beginning to evolve in new directions. This was partly a reflection of changing architectural sensibilities introduced by a new generation of architects who arrived in Singapore just after the end of the war, but it also registered changes in colonial society during the interwar period. Easily the brightest star in the new architectural firmament was one Frank Wilhim Brewer, who joined Swan & Maclaren in 1919. Although Brewer's residential work was still very much in the Arts and Crafts tradition, he drew his inspiration from rather different sources, combining the 'Cotswold vernacular' style of C. F. A. Voysey, with a dash of Charles Rennie Mackintosh and the 'Spanish mission' style of southern California.

◀▲ House for E. A. Barbour & Co. Ltd., Dalvey Estate, Frank Brewer (1927).

On the Cusp of Modernism

Frank Wilhim Brewer (1886-1971) was born in Richmond, Surrey, and was himself the son of an architect, Frank J. Brewer, FRIBA. A graduate of King's College, University of London, Brewer was the first university-trained architect to practice in Singapore. A member of the Society of Architects from 1908, Brewer automatically became a fellow of the RIBA in 1925 when the Society merged with the Institute. He was also a member of the English Art Workers' Guild, which gave him a good Arts and Crafts background.

Before the First World War, Brewer had been a partner in his father's firm, Brewer, Smith & Brewer. When war broke out, Brewer joined the Royal Engineers, rising to the rank of captain by the conclusion of hostilities. With the peace, Brewer decided to try his luck abroad and he came out East to join Swan & Maclaren in 1919.

Although Brewer's domestic architecture was rooted in the Arts and Crafts movement, his greatest influence seems to have been the Edwardian architect C. F. A. Voysey. Although Voysey was himself an Arts and Crafts man, he was a generation on from the likes of Philip Webb and William Morris and his architecture had little in common with the quasi-medieval enthusiasms of the Arts and Crafts pioneers. Distinctive Voysey features included long, low frontal elevations with the windows tucked up under the eaves, plain, unornamented, external walls in roughcast cement, and a dramatic expanse of hipped roof. All of these elements can be found in Brewer's architecture. Buttresses, which were a characteristic element of Voysey's work throughout his career, were another Brewer staple.

▲ Messrs. Sandiland Buttery & Co., Cluny Road (1923).
An early example of Brewer's mature style, this house has all the key Brewer elements: buttresses, exposed brick arches and voussoirs, half-timbered gables and a soaring roof line with flared eaves.

▶ Apartment building, Club Street (1925); Brewer's Chinese eclectic style with a dash of Charles Rennie Mackintosh thrown in for good measure.

▼ C. F. A. Voysey's material pragmatism and rejection of unnecessary ornamentation, together with his fondness for a horizontal emphasis in a manner not unlike his contemporary, Frank Lloyd Wright, are often cited as representing the connecting link between the Arts and Crafts movement and early Modernism. Certainly, there would seem to be some truth in this assertion when it comes to Singapore, in that Frank Brewer, whose houses tend to reflect the influence of the later Voysey, was also responsible for some of Singapore's finest prewar Modernist architecture, most notably, the Singapore Swimming Club (1935) and the Cathay Building (1939).

The Sandilands Buttery House

Brewer's first houses in the early-to-mid twenties may have featured half-timbered gables and other black and white elements, but Brewer was clearly heading in a different direction when he came to design his magnificent two-storey residence at Cluny Road for Messrs. Sandilands Buttery & Co. Ltd., in 1923. This is a huge place with buttressed walls, oriole windows, exposed brick voussoirs round the arches and a lot of roughcast plaster-work. The influence of Voysey is clearly evident, but Brewer is no copyist and the ensemble as a whole is innovative and distinctive in its own right.

Brewer's houses are notably much more 'English' in their manner — the Anglo-Indian references of the prewar black and white houses have all but disappeared and but for the louvred shutters and ventilation grilles, they would not look out of place in the Home Counties.

▲ Garden view of the house.

◀ The stunning front elevation of the house, effortlessly brings together disparate elements in a single coherent whole, and confirms Brewer as an early modern master, not only within a Singaporean context, but internationally too.

▼ Interior views of the entrance hall and the first-floor 'lounge verandah', which extends over the car port.

No. 1 Dalvey Estate

No. 1 Dalvey Estate is another Brewer masterwork, commissioned by E. A. Barbour & Co. in 1927. As in the case of the Sandilands Buttery house, No. 1 has all the classic Brewer hallmarks: flared eaves, buttressed walls, oriole windows and exposed brick voussoirs. Although an imposing-enough residence when viewed from the outside, the internal arrangement of rooms within is surprisingly simple — just two up, two down, with a central stairwell and the kitchen and servants' quarters detached to the rear. This impression of robustness and solidity was another characteristic aspect of Brewer's residential work, and it has been suggested that Brewer's own personal appearance might have played a role in the development of his singular architectural sensibilities. Brewer was a large man, physically — he was reputed to have been an amateur heavyweight-boxing champion in the UK before the First World War — and as Lee Kip Lin observes, "his heavy and robust style was in keeping with his build."

▶ Brewer's distinctive semi-circular window units, with an oriole window over.

▼ In recent years, No. 1 Dalvey Estate belonged to the late Mr. Ong Teng Cheong, Singapore's first elected President and himself a prominent architect. Renovations and extensions to the house by his own practice, Ong & Ong Architects Pte. Ltd., won the Urban Redevelopment Authority's Architectural Heritage Award in 2001.

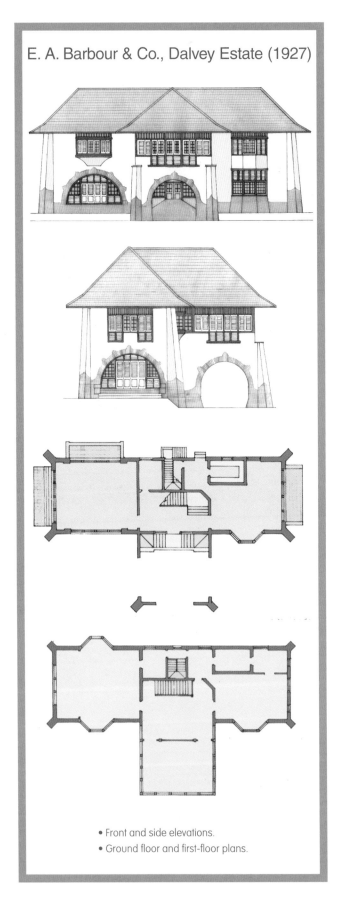

E. A. Barbour & Co., Dalvey Estate (1927)

• Front and side elevations.
• Ground floor and first-floor plans.

▲ Kitchen wing and chimney — even in the late 1920s, home cooking in Singapore was still done on an open charcoal hearth; entrance porch interior; bay window with flared base, another characteristic Brewer trademark.

▶ The front elevation, following the 2001 restoration.

MILITARY
BLACK & WHITES

THE LAST OF THE 'BLACK AND WHITES' to be built were designed mainly by and for the military, in the run-up to the Second World War. This final chapter in the black and white story began around 1935, as signs of Japan's increasing bellicosity led to a revival of Britain's plans to turn Singapore into a major naval and military base to defend British interests in the Far East. It continued up until the outbreak of the war in Europe, by which time the island of Singapore represented Britain's biggest concentration of military forces east of Suez. Not that this was sufficient to stop the Japanese when war eventually came. The fall of Singapore on 15 February 1942 was a shattering blow not only for the people of Singapore, but for the British Empire as a whole, effectively signalling the beginning of the end of Great Britain's presence as an imperial power in the Far East. It was also the end of the black and white house as an architectural tradition.

◀ Command House, Kheam Hock Road (formerly part of Sime Road) (mid-1930s).
Originally the Combined Operations Headquarters of the British Army and Air Force, Command House became the Far East Command General Headquarters during the Second Word War. General A. E. Percival, Commander-in-Chief of the Allied forces, directed the Malayan Campaign from Command House until just four days before the fall of Singapore. Architecturally, the house is interesting on account of its butterfly plan, which is clearly seen in this aerial photograph. The butterfly plan was a popular Arts and Crafts configuration Bidwell used it for Raffles Hotel in 1899 and again in his Singapore Cricket Club extension of 1907.

Black & White Barracks

The earliest purpose-built quarters for the military in Singapore were the barracks at Tanglin, which date from the mid-nineteenth century. They were most likely designed by Colonel George Chancellor Collyer of the Madras Engineers, Chief Engineer of the Straits Settlements between 1858 and 1862. The original buildings were large, airy structures, with timber floors and walls, raised on masonry piers some four or five feet above the ground. Double-leafed doors and windows were placed at regular intervals to ensure maximum through ventilation and an open verandah ran round all four sides of each building; a high, hipped *atap* roof, with broad eaves, completed the ensemble.

These early barrack buildings were modelled on the Anglo-Malay/plantation-style houses of the day and when later additions were made to the barracks between 1896 and 1907, the architects responsible — possibly the Public Works Department, or else military engineers — turned to the black and white style which was just coming into fashion at that time (the earliest PWD houses on Goodwood Hill also date from around this period). With the build-up of the military in the mid-1930s, there was a further extension of the barrack facilities and officers' quarters at Tanglin; these later additions were again modelled on contemporary buildings designed by the PWD.

▲ Tanglin Barracks in the 1890s.

The earliest barracks at Tanglin were built in the style of the contemporary Anglo-Malay plantation house. This was both a practical and economical solution — the issue of who was to pay for the defence of Singapore was always a bone of contention. At the same time, it set a precedent for subsequent military facilities in Singapore, which generally tended to be modelled on whatever was the then current bungalow style of architecture.

▼ Military building at Dempsey Road.

Note the triple-tier roof to assist ventilation of the huge roof cavity, a highly effective form of natural air-conditioning, which may originally have been borrowed from Malay architecture.

The Singapore Strategy

▲ Officers' accommodation, Winchester Road, Alexandra Park (1937). Here we see a typical example of the military-style bungalow of the mid-to-late thirties, which is clearly modelled on the archetypal black and white PWD bungalow of the mid-twenties. In this instance, the house is built directly onto the road, there being little through traffic other than vehicles belonging to the residents in house further along Winchester Road.

▼ British warship undergoing a refit in the dry dock at Sembawang, September 1940.

The strategic importance of Singapore grew rapidly after the First World War as Anglo-Japanese relations deteriorated and Japan's increasingly militaristic stance, particularly in relation to China, signalled an increasing danger in the East. In 1919, Viscount Jellicoe, who was regarded as Britain's foremost naval authority, was sent on a fact-finding mission to India and the Dominions to assess plans being made by the individual governments for both local and regional naval defence. Jellicoe, who foresaw the potential threat of the Imperial Japanese Navy, recommended the stationing of a large modern battle fleet in the Far East; Hong Kong was too vulnerable to landward assaults and Sydney was too far to the south, which left Singapore as the only viable port in the region to answer to these needs. Jellicoe described Singapore in 1919 as "undoubtedly the key to the Far East."

The so-called "Singapore Strategy" was slow in implementation, mainly on account of the huge expense involved, and it was not until 1928 that work eventually began on a naval base at Sembawang. The project was scheduled to last seven years, and, as well as docks, workshops, fuel tanks and other storage facilities, it was also envisaged that accommodation would have to be provided for some two thousand naval personnel. And the navy was just part of the military build-up in Singapore — the island's artillery and air defences were also progressively extended as part of the overall plan to turn Singapore into a "Gibraltar of the East."

Bukit Damai, Alexandra Park

Despite endless wrangles over the size of the Straits Settlements' contribution to the defence budget, work went ahead in the last decade of the nineteenth century to improve Singapore's defences. This included the building of new barracks and other military facilities to accommodate an increased military presence on the island. Alexandra Barracks, on the high ground overlooking Pasir Panjang, dates from the turn of the century and was named after Princess Alexandra, wife of the then Prince of Wales, later Edward VII. The main cantonment was to the east of Alexandra Road, with a separate site, a former pepper plantation, set aside for officers' accommodation to the west—today's Alexandra Park.

The oldest houses at Alexandra Park, excepting the so-called Plantation House on Russells Road, are Nos. 5 and 7 Royal Road, which were completed in 1906. Number 7, which goes by the name of Bukit Damai, or 'Peaceful Hill' in Malay, was built for the Commanding Officer of Alexandra Barracks and stands on the crest of a hilly ridge running through Alexandra Park, which afforded superb views in a westerly direction over the Straits of Singapore—during the Japanese Occupation the house was used as an observation post.

◀▼ Bukit Damai, Alexandra Park (1906).

Built as the residence for the Commanding Officer of Alexandra Barracks, Bukit Damai is a substantial example of tropical Edwardian architecture, comparable in style to the more or less contemporary Admiral's House at Bukit Chermin (see pp. 72-75).

▲ Entrance porch and front door.

▶ Colonnaded verandah and patio.

There was once an uninterrupted view from this side of the house, westwards across the Straits of Singapore, but new buildings along Pasir Panjang Road have spoilt the vista and made a curtain wall of foliage preferable.

Bukit Damai is foursquare in plan with a symmetrical internal arrangement of rooms in the manner of the nineteenth century. It is built over a raised basement, or plinth, with a colonnaded verandah running round three sides of the house at the ground floor level. It is a fairly robust piece of architecture which eschews the timber-frame construction more typical of the contemporary Singapore house at the turn of the century, in favour of load-bearing masonry walls. This solidity no doubt stood the occupants of the house in good stead when Bukit Damai was besieged during the Singapore mutiny of 1915. The house at that time, was the residence of Lieutenant-Colonel Edward Victor Martin, Commanding Officer of the 5th Bengal Light Infantry, garrisoned at Alexandra Barracks. On the afternoon of 15 February, when the regiment mutinied — it was falsely rumoured that they were going to be sent to Mesopotamia to fight the Turks, that is to say their fellow Muslims — Martin was holed up at Bukit Damai with three officers and a woman, the wife of a brother officer. They were subsequently joined by four officers and 81 men of the Malay States Volunteer Rifles, and together, they managed to hold off repeated attacks by the mutineers until relieved the following day.

Ridley Park

The increased military presence in Singapore from the early 1920s onwards required that existing facilities be expanded in order to accommodate the growing number of military personnel stationed on the island. When it came to providing accommodation for officers, the black and white style (as perfected by the architects of the PWD for civil servants) was again a natural choice. Ridout Road and Ridley Park, to the north and south of Tanglin Barracks respectively, were the earliest of the postwar military estates to be built, some time in the twenties, as married quarters for officers and their families. But whereas the houses designed by the PWD before the First World War had looked back to the plantation houses of the nineteenth century, the influence in this instance seems to have been more contemporary, namely that of style-leaders, Swan & Maclaren, *viz.* the asymmetric, compact plan, pared-down Classicism and absence of elaborate decorative detailing — a more masculine style for the military perhaps?

▶ No. 9 Ridley Park has an L-shaped plan; other houses from the same period retained the classic symmetrical 3-bay formula of the nineteenth century.

▼ The tall round-headed arches on either side of the *porte cochère*, with their narrow span, were a distinctive feature of the early postwar military black and whites at Ridley Park and Ridout Road.

◀▲ Interior views of No. 9 Ridley Park; an unusual feature is the large open-sided terrace on the ground floor which no doubt came in handy when entertaining large gatherings of fellow officers and their wives.

Seletar Air Base

In 1923 the British government decided to construct an airfield and seaplane base at Seletar, not far from the proposed naval base at Sembawang. It was some time before the plan was implemented, but on 10 April 1927 a certain Mr. C. E. Wood, better known as 'the man who built Seletar Air Base', arrived in Singapore to take up his appointment as Principal Works and Building Officer, Royal Air Force Far East. The task was a formidable one. The allocated site was a former rubber plantation, low-lying and marshy, with a coastal fringe of mud flats and mangrove swamp. What is more, the nearest road that was accessible by motorised transport was at Paya Lebar, some five miles distant, with nothing but jungle in between. However, the excellent Mr. Woods persevered — ably assisted by seventeen British engineers and a labour force of some five thousand Tamil coolies, plus a further fifteen hundred Chinese and Malay workers. By early 1928, some six hundred acres of land had been cleared and a million tons of earth shifted to create a fully operational flying station. Though far from complete, Seletar was nevertheless ready to receive its first visitors — four Supermarine Southampton flying boats of the RAF's Far East Flight.

▼▶ No. 1 Park Lane, Seletar Air Base (c.1930).

In addition to the aerodrome and seaplane facilities, Seletar Air Base also included coolie lines, barracks and accommodation for officers. No. 1 Park Lane seems to have been based on the tried-and-tested formula of the contemporary PWD bungalow, with its linear plan (just one room deep) and the main living floor raised up a storey on masonry piers in the manner of the plantation houses of the nineteenth century. What is truly remarkable about this particular house, though, is its extraordinary length — over two hundred feet — which is more reminiscent of a Dayak longhouse in the jungles of Borneo than the home of the commanding officer of a military air base. Whatever, the adoption of this style of architecture seems to have established a precedent for the military in Singapore, who continued to build this type of bungalow as officers' quarters right up until the outbreak of the Second World War.

Alexandra Park

The military estate at Alexandra Park evolved over half a century. The earliest houses date from around 1905/1906, whilst the most recent went up after the Second World War. A number were built for senior medical staff in the Royal Army Medical Corps in conjunction with Alexandra Military Hospital, which was completed in 1940.

Spread over some fifty years, the style of architecture naturally varies quite considerably, ranging from tropical Edwardian at Bukit Damai (see pp. 112-115) to Art Deco at No. 2 Winchester Road (p. 132). The houses on Canterbury and York Roads date from the late twenties and they are evidently based on the PWD's plantation-style houses at Goodwood Hill, Seton Close and Nassim Road (pp.54-59). No more than twenty years separate these military black and whites from their PWD forebears, but building technologies have moved on and one finds that many elements which, in the PWD houses, were made of wood — for example floor joists or ventilation grilles — are reconstituted at Alexandra Park in concrete. In terms of layout, however, the configuration is exactly the same as the houses at Nassim Road and Seton Close, right down to the location of the staircase to one side of the entrance, a design feature that ultimately can be traced right back to the middle of the nineteenth century.

◀▼ No. 4 Canterbury Road, Alexandra Park (c.1928).
The house replicates, albeit more in concrete than in wood, the half-timbered plantation-style black and white houses built by the PWD before the First World War.

An ever-increasing military presence in Singapore from the mid-thirties onwards led to a further round of building at Alexandra Park between 1936-1937. Again the PWD seems to have furnished a precedent, but whereas the earlier houses on Canterbury and York Roads looked back to plantation-style black and whites on Goodwood Hill, these later additions — the houses on Hyderabad and Winchester Roads, for example — are modelled on PWD bungalows from the mid-twenties. A characteristic feature of the latter group of houses is their positioning on the side of a slope, with the front elevation of the house being raised on brick or concrete piers and the rear of the house at ground level. No doubt the hilly topography of Alexandra Park encouraged this solution, but the origins of this style, of course, derive from the PWD houses built at Adam Park, and Malcolm and Kay Siang Roads, around 1925. The military version, however, was further simplified in terms of detailing, the half-timbered façades of the PWD houses being replaced by a reinforced concrete frame with brick in-fill.

◀ Military black and white, Winchester Road (1936).

▼ The Alexandra Park estate is notable for its superb landscaping with the roads following the natural contours of the land and the houses well spaced out with vistas across verdant swathes of open parkland, complemented by wooded valleys and leafy vales.

Sembawang Naval Base

Alexandra Park was built for the military, but similar accommodation was provided for the navy at Sembawang. Although the Sembawang houses were designed by the civil engineering firm of Sir John Jackson Ltd., who had won the contract for the naval base, the architects responsible seem to have again been looking at the back catalogue of the Public Works Department for their inspiration: the use of modern building materials such as reinforced concrete and Marseilles roof tiles aside, the standard Sembawang house ultimately derives from the PWD's prewar plantation-style prototype. There are some with unrendered brick surfaces — a nod in the direction of Frank Brewer perhaps — but even these, in their essentials, adhere to the same basic configuration.

Housing the regiment meant regimented housing and just like the civil service, one could tell a person's rank within the military or naval hierarchy by the kind of house assigned to him. For example, there are four basic types of house at Sembawang, each commensurate with a particular level of seniority within the Royal Navy. As with the PWD bungalows of the prewar era, these distinctions in rank were often no more than a difference in size. The Naval number one, however, was allocated the so-called Lutyens house off Canberra Road (today's Sembawang Country Club). It is perhaps worth pointing out here that although often attributed to the great Edwardian architect and master planner of New Delhi, Sir Edwin Landseer Lutyens (1869-1944), there is no evidence to suggest that Lutyens really did design this house — it is merely in the *style* of Lutyens.

◆ Stripped of any Classical references or unnecessary elaboration, the houses at Sembawang can appear rather dull and clumsy when compared with their erstwhile PWD forbears. Nevertheless, a closer inspection clearly reveals that they are in fact the same basic house type, albeit now dressed up in proto-Modernist clothes.

▼ A novel feature of the Sembawang houses, was the provision of air-raid shelters, a tacit recognition of the growing likelihood of war in the Far East in the mid-to-late thirties.

Fortress Changi

By 1935, the strength of the Singapore garrison had risen to over 3,000 officers and men and military-related construction works had transformed the area between Sembawang and Changi from an undeveloped, marshy bog into a sprawling conurbation of service installations that, apart from the naval base itself, boasted new concrete gun emplacements, airfields, hangars, workshops, stores, pumping stations, power stations, a hospital and barrack blocks. In addition, a range of semi-detached and detached residential units were built as accommodation for officers.

In 1938 work began on what became known as 'Fortress Changi', a redoubtable battery of heavy artillery and anti-aircraft guns to defend the eastern sea approaches to the new naval base in the Johore Straits. The latter was described by the *Sydney Morning Herald* as "The Gibraltar of the East … the bastion of British Might." Work on Fortress Changi was completed in 1941 to the accompaniment of further superlatives: "a newer, bigger and better Gibraltar, one of the most formidable concatenations of naval military and strategic power ever put together anywhere." The illusion of Fortress Changi gave an entirely unfounded, false confidence in the impregnability of Singapore. As events turned out, the naval base at Sembawang, along with Fortress Changi, which had cost £60 million and taken seventeen years to build, was destroyed without a fight.

▶ Military black and white, East Church Road, Changi (1937).

▼ Singapore's defences: anti-aircraft gun, firing practice on the eve of the Pacific war.

128

The house featured here at East Church Road, Changi, was built in 1937 and is essentially the same basic bungalow type as was first introduced by the PWD in the mid-twenties at Malcolm Road, Adam Park and Kay Siang Road. The plan is linear — just one room deep with verandahs front and back — and symmetrical about a central axis. Apart from the entrance lobby and stair hall at ground level, the main living floor of the house is raised one storey on reinforced concrete piers. The kitchen and servants' quarters at the back of the house are built on the ground but because of the sloping site, they are actually at the same level as the main part of the house. The detailing is fairly sparse, which was no doubt partly a reflection of economy and urgency, but also in keeping with a military sense of efficiency and functionality. The floors are terrazzo, and reinforced concrete is much more in evidence than in the PWD houses built a decade earlier.

▶ No. 68 East Church Road, Changi, which dates from 1937, survives in more or less original condition. Scores of houses like this, or very similar, were built by the Far East Land, Air and Sea Forces at military installations across Singapore in the late thirties, as the island's defences were reinforced to defend the new naval base at Sembawang and in anticipation of the impending war in the Pacific. Even at this late date, the kitchen was still removed from the main body of the house and cooking continued to be done on open charcoal hearths. One innovation that we see here is the 'concertina' folding shutters of the sitting room windows, which allow for unobstructed views of the garden. Interestingly, Bidwell's instructions for Atbara, back in 1898, specify the use of concertina shutters for the drawing room, but the idea did not catch on.

ART DECO
& MODERNISM

ART DECO AND MODERNIST TENDENCIES did not really begin
to make themselves felt until the 1930s. The advent of reinforced
concrete and a new generation of architects, fresh from
architectural colleges in England, helped to pave the way for
the new styles, but it was mainly the military who adopted the
new idiom. They developed a tropical Deco style of architecture,
which was found to be more appropriate, environmentally,
than out-and-out Modernism — the concrete box school of
architecture with its flat roofs and sheer façades was hardly
well-suited to Singapore's equatorial monsoon climate. In
many respects, this tropicalised Deco style was not unlike the
architecture of old Miami Beach, though this is probably more
a case of parallel evolution than any direct influence.

◀ No. 2 Winchester Road, Alexandra Park (1948).

A distinguishing feature of the new military bases built in Singapore in the runup to
the Second World War was the innovative use of reinforced concrete and Modernist
elements to create a new kind of tropical architecture for the thirties. This house at
Alexandra Park, which was actually built just after the end of the war, represents a
late example of the style.

133

Tropical Deco

The influence of the modern movement did not really make an impact on the domestic architecture of Singapore until the early thirties. Interestingly, the style was favoured more by Asian clients and Asian architects. The first generation of professionally-qualified local architects tended to have an engineering background; they may have been more comfortable with the still relatively new medium of reinforced concrete and, at the same time, less bound by convention than their European counterparts who were more likely to have studied for a degree in architecture. Whatever, the colonial house was evolving too, shedding its Anglo-Indian past in favour of a more contemporary European flavour. The verandah was superceded by terraces and patios, glazed windows replaced louvred shutters and bamboo chicks, and the kitchen moved indoors. The military were more enterprising, and the years leading up to the Second World War saw the emergence of an entirely new kind of tropical architecture in Singapore, executed in a quasi-Modernist idiom, reminiscent of South Beach, Miami. Although the style was mainly reserved for administrative buildings, one can find one or two houses at Ridley Park, Alexandra Park and Changi, with flat roofs, rounded corners, projecting sun shades, or *soleil brisé*, and various other Art Deco embellishments. The flats for non-commissioned officers on the Portsdown Road estate are also in this tropical Deco style.

▲ This two-storey house at Peel Road, probably dates from around 1935 and shows a transitional style between the old black and white bungalows of the interwar years and the new, quasi-Art Deco/early Modernist houses of the mid-to-late thirties. The house is much more closed in than previously, while structurally, the timber-frame construction technique — which had served the Singapore house since the middle of the nineteenth century — has been superceded by a composite frame of brick piers and concrete beams with brick in-fill. There are also stylistic innovations too, notably the reinforced-concrete, Deco-style sun shades or *soleil brisé*, but notice the rather quaint anachronism in the form of a Gothic-style front door.

▼ Royal Air Force HQ, Seletar Air Base (1931).

The new naval, military and air force installations erected in the 1930s provide plenty of interesting examples of the tropical Art Deco/early Modernist style of military architecture which emerged in Singapore in the years leading up to the war in the Pacific.

▲ East Church Road, Changi (late 1930s).

In their essentials, these later houses for the military still hark back to the PWD bungalow archetype of the mid-twenties in terms of their symmetrical plan and elevations. They look modern all right, but appearances can be deceptive, and these tropical Deco villas of the late 1930s actually represent a last gasp of the black and white tradition, albeit decked out in fancy new clothes.

◀ Military flats, Portsdown Road (late 1930s).

Set in verdant surroundings the Hampshire regiment responsible for the Portsdown Road camp was noted for finding good sites and landscaping them well the tropical-Deco-style Portsdown Road apartments are to be given a new lease of life by Singapore's Urban Redevelopment Authority as artisans' studios.

135

International Style

The last prewar houses to be built at Ridley Park, with their dazzling white façades, clean lines and curved surfaces, relieved of all decorative embellishments, are just about as far-removed from the original Arts-and-Crafts-inspired black and white house of the turn of the century as it is possible to get. Indeed, some would argue that the only thing 'black and white' about them is the paintwork. But like Bidwell's Atbara or the house for Rowland Allen by Williams & Draper, they are reflections of the spirit of the age, and that spirit, or *zeitgeist*, in the late thirties, was the quasi-divine ideology of Functionalism, as promulgated by the high priests of the new International Style, Walter Gropius, Mies van der Rohe and Le Corbusier. In the case of the Ridley Park houses, the particular influence here seems to be that of the Weissenhofsiedlung — literally, 'white house estate' — in Stuttgart, which was erected in 1927 as an exhibition of workers' housing under the direction of Mies van der Rohe, and included contributions from Gropius, Le Corbsier and other leading luminaries of the Modern movement. Ultimately, I'm not sure whether these Modernist villas at Ridley Park can properly be included in the black and white canon — there is little to connect them with the other houses we have considered here, either conceptually or in terms of their execution — but as the last houses to be built by the British before the cataclysm of 1942, they provide an apposite point at which to close this study of the black and white Singapore house. This was what the future was going to look like, back in 1940 or thereabouts: ahistorical, international, and anonymous; the era of the black and white house was over.

▼▶ Kay Siang Road, Ridley Park (c.1940): the shock of the new!
Little more than forty years separate this house from Atbara but the plastic possibilities of reinforced concrete would have astounded Bidwell and his peers.

136

BLACK & WHITE
LIFESTYLES

THE ERA OF THE BLACK AND WHITE HOUSE arrived with the twentieth century and lasted up until the Japanese invasion in 1942. In 1900, Singapore was still governed primarily by mercantile interests and her leading citizens, if they were not members of the colonial administration, were typically men of commerce — bankers, businessmen, commodity brokers, shipping magnates and financiers. It was a cosmopolitan society — prosperous and rapidly growing in size — and seemingly on the verge of even greater things. Malayan tin was booming, oil was becoming an increasingly important commodity and the rubber revolution was just around the corner.

Doctors, barristers and the *tuan besars* (lit. 'big lords') of the large commercial houses—these were the men who, when they could afford it, would buy a plot of land, often a couple of acres or more, somewhere at the upper end of Orchard Road (Grange Road, Leonie Hill and the Cluny Estate or Tanglin were the most sought-after districts) and then commission one of Singapore's small but flourishing architectural practices to design a house for them — Swan & Maclaren, led by the talented Mr. Bidwell, was the practice of choice. And just as in England, where a prosperous middle-class businessman or professional would have opted for something vaguely Tudoresque in manner, so too in Singapore — the *beau ideal* of the English country gentleman was as strong in the Straits Settlements as ever it was in Surrey or Middlesex.

◀ Afternoon tea on the lawn, c.1900; note the adoption of the Malay *sarong* as informal attire around the house.

Verandah Living

In the days before electricity and the advent of the electric fan, life was lived very much on the verandah. The latter often extended round all four sides of the house, which helped protect the core of the building from the warming effect of solar radiation, while at the same time providing light and breezy communal areas for its occupants to pass the day. Tiled floors, high ceilings and large openings kept these spaces cool and encouraged the circulation of air, while bamboo blinds or chicks cut down the glare and shielded the verandah itself from direct sunlight. Cane furniture and maidenhair ferns, drooping decoratively from jardinières, completed the picture, making the verandah a welcome and restive place to retreat to from the fierce heat of the midday tropic sun. As Jan Morris observes in her *Stones of Empire*, the verandah was "the one place imperialists had just for messing around."

▶ Sitting verandah, Nassim Road.

The first-floor sitting verandah, extending out over the *porte cochère*, was the focal point of domestic life in the black and white house — just the place to retire to in the cool of the evening to enjoy a whiskey *ayer* (whiskey and water) or a gin *pahit* (gin and bitters) as the lengthening shadows steal across a well-manicured lawn. Or after dinner, for a postprandial brandy with friends, the table lamps throwing a rosy glow over the proceedings, the garden, now dark and mysterious, out there beyond the comforting pool of light, while someone sits down at the piano to play a Chopin nocturne.

▼ *The London Illustrated News*, albeit a month late, and billiards — staples of a colonial lifestyle during the era of the black and white house.

Cookboys and Amahs

In an average European household during the pre-First World War era, the typical retinue of servants would have included a cookboy and his wife, who was usually the housekeeper or *amah*; a laundry maid or 'wash-*amah*'; a nanny (*ayah*) for the children; a *tukang ayer* to keep the water jars filled in the bathrooms and to empty the commode; a gardener (*kebun*); a groom or *syce* and a night-watchman or *jaga*. Household servants tended to be Chinese from the island of Hainan, though the cookboy more often than not was from Canton as the Cantonese were meant to be the best in this department.

Domestic servants, whose household duties might require them to be called upon at any hour of the day or night, lived on the property, though in separate quarters at the back of the house, and if there were any children belonging to them, they might be employed to do some useful task like weeding the tennis court or raking the driveway. The kitchen was also out the back, again detached from the main part of the house, but connected by a covered walkway. Cooking facilities were fairly rudimentary, even as late as the 1930s, comprising a series of little brick-built fireplaces arranged in a row, the wood or charcoal fuel being fed in the front while the *wok* or cook pot rested on a circular aperture at the top. Smoke was removed by a flue, and if one walks round the back of any surviving black and white house today, one can still see a chimney protruding from the roof of the kitchen annex, a somewhat incongruous sight in such a tropical setting as Singapore.

▲ 'Black and white' *amahs*, with their charges.

The legendary black and white *amahs* from Canton — so-called because of their distinctive uniform comprising a white cotton *samfu* top over black satin trousers — were more than simply a perfect complement to the black and white house. They were renowned throughout the region for their honesty, loyalty, industry and the excellence of their service. They were much sought-after as nannies and domestic servants and once having found employment with a sympathetic family, they often stayed with that family for their entire working lives.

▼ The kitchens and servants' quarters were invariably detached from the main body of the house but connected by a covered way. The placing of the servants' accommodation a little away from the main house afforded a certain degree of privacy during off-duty hours for both employer and employee alike.

▲ A corner of the kitchen annex at No. 7 Goodwood Hill, with the garage and *syce*'s quarters beyond (above left); stables and outhouses, Mount Pleasant (above right). The motorcar did not really begin to take off in Singapore until the mid-twenties, and the era of the black and white house belonged primarily to the age of the horse-drawn vehicle.

▼ A European family out for a drive in their landau, with a Malay *syce* at the reins (below left). A round of the Botanic Gardens in one's conveyance was a popular evening pastime, pausing to enjoy the musical entertainment afforded by the bandstand. Only the well-to-do maintained an equipe with horses; the rest made do with wiry little ponies imported from Java or the Celebes (Sulawesi).

Malay *tukang kebun* (below right). Note the design of his broom, which is perfectly adapted to extricating fallen leaves from between potted plants without damaging the bloom or foliage; the same kind of broom can be seen to this day in Singapore in the hands of road sweepers and park attendants.

The *syce* and the *kebun* were usually Malay, and the *jaga*, Indian. As likely as not, they too lived on the property, to be called upon whenever some extra assistance was required in the house. With the advent of the motorcar the *syce* became the chauffeur, but although the first motorcar was imported into Singapore as early as 1896, car-ownership did not become widespread for at least another two decades. Even after the First World War, when there were 1,317 motor vehicles registered in Singapore, the great majority of European residents in the Orchard Road area still travelled to work by rickshaw. George Peet, who joined *The Straits Times* as a junior reporter in 1923, describes the daily commute: " hundreds of rickshaws in a column along Orchard Road as far as the eye could see, moving at a spanking pace towards the city, and each of them with a white-suited and topee'd passenger sitting under the hood."

House and Garden

A large part of the charm of black and white houses lies in their setting — typically on rising ground or at the summit of a modest eminence, a swathe of green lawn in front with a dark wall of trees behind, dense thickets of jungle undergrowth, a tall stand of *nibong* palms, their feathery fronds silhouetted against the sky. The dominant idea here was that of the 'garden house.' The term 'garden house' had been coined in British India, where an elegant residence set in spacious grounds was seen as appropriate recompense for a life 'in exile'. Garden houses could be found stretched along the esplanades in Madras and Calcutta in the nineteenth century, and they provided the archetype for the colonial house in Singapore and the Straits Settlements. In terms of the actual landscaping, the park-like setting was quite consciously modelled on the English country estate, that is to say, in the eighteenth-century manner of William Kent and Capability Brown. The perimeter of the property was typically planted up with dense vegetation which provided privacy from one's neighbours and passers-by, while the layout of the garden was informally arranged with stands of trees — *tembusu* (*Fragraea fragrans*) was a popular choice — separated by undulating lawns and brightly-coloured flower beds planted with canna lilies, orchids and the ubiquitous Heliconia in all its myriad forms. A long driveway, cut between mossy banks and ferns, led up to the house where one alighted from one's carriage or automobile in the shade of the *porte cochère*. In the case of the government and corporate estates, the houses were typically grouped together in little enclaves, the low-rise forerunner of today's condominium lifestyle.

▶ Tennis and squash courts, Alexandra Park (right, top and middle).
A great deal of social life during the black and white era revolved around sporting activities, either at home or at 'the club'. Tennis parties were especially popular. J. D. Ross, writing in 1898, observed that "the amount of tennis played in Singapore is something astonishing. " This was deemed to be no bad thing, for "all this promotes social relations between the sexes."

▶ Driveway at Temenggong Road (right, bottom).
A black and white house without its garden would be like a ship on dry land. Gardening was an enthusiasm embraced by many a colonial *mem*, encouraged no doubt by Singapore's super-luxuriant tropical vegetation and colourful flora. Of course, it was also handy that arduous tasks like digging flower beds could be safely delegated to the *kebun*.

▶▶ PWD bungalow, Nassim Road (c. 1910) — verdant lawns and mature stands of trees — the archetypal setting of the black and white house.

144

Index

ACKNOWLEDGMENTS

Many people generously gave their time and help to make this book possible, not least the people who live in the beautiful houses which are featured here and whose names are given below — to all of them, a big thank you. I should also like to thank the staff at the National Archives of Singapore for their kind assistance over many years. In particular, I would like to thank the former Head of Reference, Pauline Phua, without whose enthusiasm and hard work much of the research for this book would not have been possible. I should also like to thank her successor, Ms. Wong Wee Hon, who was most helpful when it came to putting together the archival materials that are reproduced in the book. Thanks are also due to Dr. George Caldwell and to Brian Farrell, Associate Professor of Military History at the National University of Singapore, for their useful comments and suggestions. Thank you, too, to Helen West for help with archival sources relating to the houses, their owners, and the architects who built them. Last, but by no means least, a big thank you to the team at Talisman, and in particular, my editor, Ian Pringle, who helped to make this book considerably more focused than it might have been.

With special thanks to the President and Committee of the Singapore Heritage Society.

The Residents:
Shelley Adams, Miranda and Dominic Armstrong, Nathalie Baseden, Victoria Brown, Maureen Callahan, Carol Church, James Crawford, Jeanette and Bernard Eschweiler, Joyce and Nol van Fenema-Tulkens, Debbie and Neil Franks, Jack Garity, Lucinda and Philip Hampden-Smith, Normi and Alistair Hazell, Claudia and Hogi Hyun, Barbara Iversen, Charlotte Marson, Karen McCulloch, Karen and Mark Nelligan, Teresa and Ryan Padgett, Christine and Peter Taylor, Shauna and Eric Varvel, John Venning, Pauline and Steven West, Thomas Zilliacus, Aprim Interior Design.

PICTURE CREDITS

All illustrations by the author, except for p. 30, Derek Corke.

Photographs by Luca Invernizzi Tettoni, except for:
Antiques of the Orient p. 28; Australian War Memorials p. 111 (bottom); Cable & Wireless p. 65, pp. 76-77; *Country Life* p. 36; Julian Davison p. 20, p. 69, p. 71, p. 89 (top), p. 142 (top right); Imperial War Museum, London p. 128; Lee Kip Lin p. 17, p. 140; Lim Kheng Chye p. 100 (left); Gretchen Liu p. 110 (top); National Archives of Singapore p. 15, p. 48, p. 54, p. 88, p. 100 (right), p. 134 (top), p. 142 (top left), p. 143 (bottom right); Ong & Ong Architects Pte Ltd pp. 98-99, p. 101, p. 104, pp. 105-107; Guido Rossi pp. 108-109; Singapore History Museum pp. 138-139, p. 143 (bottom left); Douglas Wain-Heapy p. 34 (bottom).

Other images: Antiques of the Orient pp. 10-11, p. 14 (bottom); British Library p. 14 (top); National Archives of Singapore pp. x-xi, pp. 38-39, p. 49 (middle and bottom), p. 70, p. 71, p. 78, pp. 80-81, p. 88; Luca Invernizzi Tettoni p. 12.

Regent Alfred John Bidwell
1869 – 1918